TRENDS & ISSUES

IN SECONDARY ENGLISH

2000 EDITION

NATIONAL COUNCIL OF TEACHERS OF ENGLISH
1111 W. KENYON ROAD, URBANA, ILLINOIS 61801-1096

Staff Editor: Bonny Graham
Interior Design: Tom Kovacs for TGK Design; Carlton Bruett
Cover Design: Carlton Bruett

NCTE Stock Number: 55146-3050
ISSN 1527-425X

TRENDS AND ISSUES

Keeping track of the myriad issues in education can be a daunting task for those educators already stretched to fit thirty hours into a twenty-four-hour day. In an effort to inform and support English educators, the National Council of Teachers of English annually offers this volume featuring current trends and issues deemed vital to the professional conversation by our membership at large. Whether specialists or generalists, teachers know that no single "trend" or "issue" could touch the interests and concerns of all members of NCTE; with these books—one for each section of the Council: Elementary, Secondary, Postsecondary—we aim to chronicle developments in the teaching and learning of English language arts.

The wealth of NCTE publications from which to draw the materials for *Trends and Issues* proves a double-edged sword. Publishing thirteen journals (bimonthly and quarterly) and twenty to twenty-five books annually provides ample content, yet what to include and what not? Of course, timeliness and pertinence to the issues of the day help shape the book, and, more important, we aim to meet our primary goal: to answer the question, Is this valuable to our members? This edition of *Trends and Issues* offers readers a seat at the table, a chance to join the discussion. At the postsecondary level, the trends and issues cited for this year are "Race/Class/Gender Positions," "Technology," and "Writing Assessment." At the secondary level, members cited "The World Wide Web in the Classroom," "The Reemergence of Critical Literacy," and "Aesthetic Appreciation versus Critical Interrogation" as those topics of current relevance to them as English language arts professionals. At the elementary level, the trends and issues encompass "Writing and a Move to New Literacies," "Critical Literacy," and "Taking New Action."

We hope that you'll find this collection a valuable resource to be returned to often, one that facilitates professional development and reminds us that we all have a stake in the language arts profession.

NCTE invites you to send us those trends and issues in the English language arts that you feel are the most relevant to your teaching. Send your comments either to our Web site at www.ncte.org or e-mail directly to Dale Allender at dallender@ncte.org.

Dale Allender
Associate Executive Director

CONTENTS

III. Aesthetic Appreciation versus Critical Interrogation

INTRODUCTION

Trends and issues of all sorts surfaced and helped shape the 2000 teaching year. Thoughtful identification and consideration of these issues by NCTE's six commissions brought forth increased attention to interactions of race, class, language and learning, the pitfalls of high-stakes testing, English-language development, the need to attend to pedagogy when building a multicultural literature curriculum, and the importance of media literacy as primary concerns among English language arts educators at all levels. Similarly, the NCTE Committee on Resolutions has identified diversity, broadly speaking; high-stakes testing; bilingual education; and government intrusion into teachers' professional decision making as issues needing the attention of the English language arts profession.

While the commissions survey the field at large to broadly gauge the profession, and the Committee on Resolutions considers specific positions that NCTE should take on a variety of contemporary English language arts issues, this volume examines periodical and nonperiodical publications of the National Council of Teachers of English as an additional method of assessing topics important to teachers at the secondary level.

Among the dozens of journal articles and book chapters published this year, three important topics have emerged, forming here the organizing sections of this collection: The World Wide Web in the Classroom; The Reemergence of Critical Literacy; and Aesthetic Appreciation versus Critical Interpretation. The use of technology, and specifically the Internet, continues to expand the range of instructional possibility. The introduction and evolution of the Internet in the classroom highlights the importance of English language arts educators' role in preparing students to become critically literate members of our democratic society. Finally, while the "art for art's sake" versus the "art as political expression" debate has continued for many years, our writers bring fresh, new pedagogical nuance to the discussion.

PERMISSIONS

I The World Wide Web in the Classroom

Most U.S. high schools in some way use computer technology. Teaching and administering education has become an electronic enterprise. Judith L. Scott's article provides a transition and introduction to understanding the use of the Internet in the classroom at the beginning of this millennium: a transition for veteran teachers whose teacher training did not prepare them for this digital revolution, and an introduction for the novice educator who has electronic savvy but little teaching experience. Ted Nellen then details the dynamic, student-centered nature of the World Wide Web as a writing-instruction tool, elaborating on structural and instructional uses of the Internet in his classroom, such as posting the class syllabus on the Web and giving specific assignments that involve research and writing via the Internet. Jean Boreen describes a university summer class she teaches that explores practical uses of the Internet as a writing and research tool for middle-level students. A primary goal of the class is to demonstrate how the Internet can be a motivating tool for student engagement. Toward this end, the class is taught as a mixed-grade experience, with students ranging from middle school through university level, including some veteran teachers.

While many who write about technology highlight the advantages of this new and expansive tool, few note pitfalls or offer caution. Susan A. Gardner, Hiltraut H. Benham, and Bridget M. Newell point out how fallible the Internet can be in the research process, and provide guidelines for evaluating Internet sources. Albert B. Somers's "Poetry and the Internet" evaluates Web pages, discussion groups, electronic journals, and a variety of other resources on the Internet all related to poetry and the teaching of poetry.

1 Journey into Cyberspace

Judith L. Scott

The excitement in the air is almost palpable as we prepare for this journey into the new millennium. The world is awash with expectations, teeming with enthusiasm and anticipation for the years ahead. Approaching this millennium mark has taken, well, a millennium(!) but, for me, packing will take but a moment. Give me a laptop and offer me a window seat and I'm ready. My laptop will carry the technology my students need not only to survive but to thrive on the new information highway and the window seat will give me a vantage point as I look out in wonder on an educational future filled with promise.

Looking back on the past decade, it would be fair to say that the emergence of technology was truly unfair. After all, those of us who began our teaching careers before the '80s could not have anticipated the Electronic Classroom. We were pleased with a media repertoire that included chalkboards, mimeograph machines, spirit duplicators, overhead projectors, and an occasional filmstrip. But now, in the classroom of the new millennium, we are expected to talk in acronyms such as www, CD-ROM, and LCD. For many of us, that's scary language and requires courage some of us aren't sure we've got. Remember Prometheus, that good-intentioned demi-god whom the Greeks credit with putting fire into the hands of humans? Well, he has nothing on the courageous classroom teacher who dares to put a group of eighth graders in a computer lab linked to the Internet.

Until the emergence of technology, the classroom seemed a predictable place where teachers taught and students learned. It its understandable, then, that some of us think technology has turned the world upside down.

Reprinted from *Voices from the Middle*, December 1999.

Today our students, the inheritors of the computer age, are often steps ahead of us. Undaunted by fear or limitation, they venture into cyberspace where, for better or for worse, they are willing to go where most teachers have not gone before.

Not since Guttenberg invented the printing press have educators been asked to make such a monumental change. It seems that John Naisbitt, author of Megatrends, was right when, in the early 1980s, he claimed "that in the information society, the two required languages will be English and computer" (Naisbitt, p. 29). Technology, with all its challenges and unresolved questions, has indeed survived the litmus test of the '90s. Those of us willing to accept the challenge are left with the reality that we must determine not "if" but "how" technology will be used in the classroom.

If we agree that technology is here to stay, then the answer to how technology will be used begins with our willingness and ability to take advantage of this incredible tool. To do this, I'll suggest, just as Atwell suggested with her workshop approach to literacy (Atwell, 1998), that our job is less to tell than to show, less to dispense than to support, less to insist than to assist. Furthermore, we must be willing to go through cyberspace with our students, learning with them how technology affects our knowledge. Finally, we must be willing to let go of the overhead projector and try the computer monitor.

In the classroom of the late 1990s, we teachers are just beginning to separate the reality from the promise. We've come to understand that technology, with all its glitz and glamour, is a cog in the wheel of education—not the wheel itself. Technology-savvy language arts teachers, for example, have found the computer, when used in conjunction with a presentation device such as an LCD panel or a TV/computer connection, to be an ideal vehicle for group brainstorming, pre-writes, and minilessons. Tools such as Internet hyperlinks, virtual fieldtrips, interactive reviews, and multimedia presentations are adding a new dimension to lesson plans—not replacing them.

In classrooms where teachers understand how to let technology assist them, students are learning more. Researchers at the U.S. Department of Education have found that technology use results in better student attitudes toward learning and that students tend to be more cooperative and interactive in their learning when technology is added. Computers support team concepts and group interaction that generally result in students operating on higher levels of thinking and problem solving (http://gsu.edu/dept/academic/EDU/projects/technology/ Resources.htm).

Futurists such as Naisbitt look to the past to examine the journey so far and therefore predict the future of technology. Through their research we have learned that fifth-grade students have been exposed to more information than their grandparents were exposed to in a lifetime. In fact, the total amount of knowledge is doubling every 18 months. Eighty-five percent of what we teach today will change or be proven wrong in the next century (http://gsu.edu/dept/academic/EDU/projects/technology/session_1/s0101.htm).

The education our students will need for tomorrow requires that we teach differently today. The literacy skills for the 21st century will require each student to be a discriminating information seeker as well as a competent communicator. Students will need to obtain the skills necessary to decipher and analyze data from an ever-growing well of sources. They will need to understand how to separate and substantiate the information offered from sources that may not be required to meet a quality standard. Making sense of this vast amount of information will require a different way of examining and synthesizing data.

In the new millennium, the process of online research will replace the delivery of printed facts. The dilemma of how to replace outdated textbooks will be resolved by the use of less costly, easily updateable CD-ROMs as well as online links that textbook companies will most likely provide. Students will have the flexibility to pursue topics anywhere and anytime as the portable laptop computer and wireless technology replace notebooks and desktop computers.

Victor Hugo said, "Nothing is so powerful as an idea whose time has come." Just as television changed our perception of the world in this century, technology will change our perception of education in the 21st century. Video conferencing and distance learning through satellite technology promise to topple the walls of the cubical classroom and make the "global classroom" a reality. Students will have access to the brightest minds and the most current information on every subject imaginable.

Keeping up with the pace set by technology can be a difficult task—but keeping up is essential. Just as the advent of the Gutenberg press caused a wave of literacy that separated the masses into literate and illiterate, technology will inevitably have a similar effect. The grace period of the past quarter century is over. Today technology is not optional for educators; it's required.

So, as I prepare for my journey into the new millennium, I will insist only that technology be my essential carry-on. With laptop in hand, I will look out the window toward the new millennium, imagining a literacy journey that promises to be both challenging and rewarding.

References

Atwell, N. (1998). *In the middle: New understandings about writing, reading, and learning.* Portsmouth, NH: Heinemann.

Naisbitt, J. (1988). *Megatrends.* New York: Warner.

2 Using the Web for High School Student Writers

Ted Nellen

By today's pedagogical standards, I am a Constructivist. I have been one since my first days as a teacher of writing in 1974. I have always believed the Deweyan idea that we learn by doing, and having my students do is the best way to have my students learn how to learn. My classroom is student-centered, not teacher-centered. Watching students work out problems in groups or in isolation is education at its best. Constructivists use this term because students construct a solution on their own or in collaboration with others. To best illustrate my constructivist point of view, I direct you to my students' homepages at http://199.233.193.1/work.html. Their work is organized by student and by assignment.

The World Wide Web provides the perfect environment for the writing process. I believe this because the Web transcends desktop publishing and presentation programs. The Web provides a student writer with complete control over the creation, from inspiration to publication. Student writers have a wider audience, a more democratic audience, and a venue for peer review when they use the Internet. However, once access is achieved, the next question is what do I do? I will attempt to provide the reader with some insights about how I have transformed a traditional writing class into a Webbed writing class. I will provide a glimpse of our students and the electrified environment, the Web tools we use and how we use them, the Webfolio (or wired portfolio), and student Web writing results and teacher resources.

Reprinted from Chapter 16 of *Weaving a Virtual Web*, edited by Sibylle Gruber.

Electrifying the Environment

The 3,200 students in our school (http://199.233.193.1/) are a heterogeneous group picked from the population of every district in New York City. The age range is from 13 to 18. A third are Asian, a third are African American, and a third are Hispanic/Latino. The hallways are alive with the non-English languages which many call their mother tongues. The Internet is ideal for these students. My classroom (http://199.233.193.1/comprms.html#439) has thirty-four computers connected to the Internet. In the classic Lancasterian mode, I have interns and colleagues-in-training who help manage the room. The interns are students from the previous year who assist the new students and teachers in some of the technical aspects of the class. This is my teacher-training model. Colleagues who wish to use the Internet in their classes also assist during my classes. By working in an active class rather than in the sterile workshop, the teacher-in-training will learn more effectively and quickly. My English class has become a real and virtual community.

I teach Cyber English (http://199.233.193.1/cybereng/), a junior-year course. The students are from special education, deaf and hard of hearing, bilingual, and mainstream populations. The only students I do not have are the honor students. The syllaweb (http://199.233.193.1/cybereng/log.html) is Internet-based. We include all of the elements of any other junior-level English class, except we work exclusively on the Internet. The students work with all genres: poetry, fiction, nonfiction, and drama. Each student contructs a Web page which becomes his or her Web portfolio, or Webfolio. The Webfolio is the key to the success of the class. The Webfolio is the homepage, each student's own page. It empowers each student, and each student has a stake in his or her own education.

I use the Internet in my classroom because it solves so many problems, bridges so many gulfs, inspires so many fertile minds, provides so much information, introduces such a large audience. The Internet is the ultimate presentation format for our students because each student becomes a publisher. The Internet provides the teacher of writing with access to the students' work right from the start and throughout the writing process. I or anyone else can access the student's work through the Web page from anywhere at any time. Since I have more access to my young student writers' work, I can be more effective as a writing teacher. There are drawbacks, however, to creating a Webbed environment. I have worked hard to connect the classroom and its thirty-four computers to the Internet. I needed lots of help from technicians who created a LINUX/UNIX server for me. It took me an entire summer to set all of this up with the IP address for the school, setting up the computers, and preparing the class. In addition, I spend a lot of time maintaining the Internet connection, preparing classes, and grading papers. I would say I spend twice as much time at my craft now than I did before I had all of this "power." So please be warned.

The Web Process

Each student creates a Web page, which is a table of contents for his or her projects. The homepage is such a powerful motivator; the students take great pride in their homepages and in their written work. Like a garden, the homepage demands constant care. By the end of the year, each student has an outstanding Webfolio which reflects his or her work for the year. Webfolios take the writing process to another level: publishing. The publishing process incorporates the writing process and considers the elements of layout: graphics, designs, color, font, presentation, hypertext. Publishing is the ultimate goal for any writer.

The Syllaweb and the Webfolio

The students follow a syllaweb (http://199.233.193.1/cybereng/log. html), an online syllabus accessed through an Internet browser, which explains and serves projects. The Webfolio is the final Web created by each student that introduces the year's work to the reading public.

The students start with three projects that help identify the writer: a short autobiography, a poem about the Internet, and a book report about their favorite book. Much of the students' personalities pour out in a short time in this new medium. After they become comfortable with Web writing, I request that they do three or four of the projects at the same time while maintaining their homepages. These projects include their own poetry, short stories, and hypertext essays. The syllaweb reflects the wide range of choices from the classic literature found in most anthologies, classic literature not found in anthologies, and literature not yet canonized. Using relevant material makes for more receptive students who in turn enjoy and retain what they have learned. I am concerned with creating students who learn how to learn, who learn to enjoy reading and writing, and my approach appears to work well: my students actually do *learn*, and they perform admirably on state standardized tests.

Specific Web Projects

Hypertext essays make every assignment a research paper. The value of using the Internet to publish student work is that the research done to create the essay was done on the Internet, hence hypertext links to the research source can more readily be made by the reader. Each Web project entails Internet research, Internet hypertext links to sources, and publishing. One such assignment used an editorial written in an online college student magazine (http://www.trincoll.edu/tj/tj9.25.95/articles/violence.html) which addressed violence in America. After the students read the editorial, they immediately went on a hunt for more information on violence. They used popular Web search engines (http: //199.233.193.1/find.html) like Yahoo, WebCrawler, Lycos, Excite, and others to find articles on violence. The students used the editorial as the basis for their own essays and then used the Internet resources to augment the editorial. In their research they went beyond U.S. borders as they sought information on African female genitalia mutilation, Bosnia, China, South America, and other areas of violence around the world. Their essays (http://199.233.193.1/ce-violence.html) were well done because of their ability to follow relevant links. The essays they eventually wrote had hypertext links back to the articles they had read which had given them the ideas they used in their papers. Hypertext adds so much to writing because the reader can immediately access the resource the writer used to verify or to learn more about the topic; sources are just a click away. It is far superior to the traditional research paper which merely refers to an article the reader then has to seek out in a library. The publishing of the essays brought in a great deal of mail praising and supporting the students' efforts. These kudos served as fuel for my students to continue.

Another successful assignment dealt with the December holidays (http://199.233.193.1/cybereng/09.html). The students researched Christmas, Hanukkah, and Kwanzaa. Again the students sought out the information on the Internet. This multicultural essay could never have been done successfully in a traditional classroom. Hypertext essays give the reader access to the writer's sources, which makes for more authentic writing and reading. These essays became part of the database for other students trying to find out information on the three holidays. It came as quite a shock when my students received letters from other students who asked them about the holidays. My students had suddenly become experts and were being asked questions as they had asked others.

Perhaps one of the most exciting projects for the students was the Cyber Biographies (http://199.233.193.1/cybereng/05.html). This project had them research the people responsible for our cyber community. Since most of these people are both alive and Internet-active, the students were able to visit these folks' homepages. Some bold students even wrote e-mail to some of these cyber pioneers. When mail came back, the students were ecstatic. Publishing on the Web made this interaction possible. As the students were able to access homepages of their subjects, the subjects in turn were able to view the students' Web pages. In addition, these cyber biographies become resource material for future student researchers.

The project which draws the most moans and complaints is the short story project (http://199.233.193.1/cybereng/13.html). The students have to read a classic short story online and then write an essay. They then have to compare and contrast a classic short story with a contemporary short story. Finally, they have to write their own short story. When I introduce them to this project, I am met with a great deal of resistance. However, I let them know that they may write any short story they wish, as long as the stories are not obscene. Living in New York City gives my students plenty of fodder for their own short stories, which are fantastic and great reads. It has become their favorite project of the year. The response to their creations draws the greatest amount of mail. Publishing on the Web gives the students access to a great deal of information and it provides the world access to the students' work. This two-way information flow is a powerful motivator.

A financial by-product of their Web presence is job offers. Publishing Web pages introduces them to potential employers. This necessitates creating an online resume (http://199.233.193.1/cybereng/17.html). Since this is a Web resume rather than a traditional resume, many considerations have to be made. This project is a real problem-solving type of situation because it involves more advanced HTML writing, like tables, and it requires students to transfer their previous knowledge of paper format to Web format. This is the first step in converting from traditional format to Web format on such a serious and important level. Students accept this transfer more easily than adults do. For the students, publishing their resumes has brought job interviews and jobs.

The students were hooked after the first day when we started their homepages. They became addicts when they started receiving mail about their homepages. Introducing the students to the Web was never difficult, and getting them to do the work is no challenge. The biggest problem is getting them to leave when the bell rings so the next class can begin work. Attendance is always close to 100 percent, and we never have an empty computer seat, because students without a class come to work. When school starts the next year, one of the students' first stops is to log on, check mail,

and to fix some of their work on their Web pages. Many former students
spend a great deal of time rewriting essays, adjusting their resumes, adding
new papers to their Web pages. They do this knowing the new work will not
affect a grade; they do it because they recognize the power of a published
Web page. Some may call it pride.

Publishing Produces Better Writers

The Internet enhances the writing process because the Internet provides the
writer, for the first time in the history of education, the power to publish his
or her work. Publishing is the power; history tells us this. As the teacher, I
can access students' work in progress from any computer connected to the
Internet. The teacher is no longer the sole audience: by publishing on the
Internet, my students benefit from "telementors," people from all walks of life
who discover the students' work, comment on it, and offer them advice. My
constructivist pedagogy is satisfied on the Internet.

One of the purposes of writing is to verify what the writer knows. When
we write something down, we sort out our knowledge and then we present
it. Writing is thinking before speaking and ultimately publishing. An example
of this epiphany for the young writer is when he or she sits with a writing
teacher and tries to explain what was meant in a recent essay. At some point
the teacher asks, "What exactly are you trying to say here?" The student
immediately breaks into a long discourse on what was meant by that vague
sentence. When the teacher can get a word in, the advice is to put this
rambling on paper. The writing process is that activity which reveals to the
writer his or her knowledge on a topic culminating in publishing.

Student publishing is successful because the teacher, peers, and mentors
can monitor the young writer's progress at any point. This constant access
allows the teacher to intervene earlier and more often in the writing process.
Mistakes are not repeated incessantly because they are caught early. Good
habits are instilled early in the writing process, eliminating the "red-ink
shock syndrome." Previously, a student might have invested a lot of time in a
paper, only to be disappointed when I returned it with a low grade. Now, I
begin looking at work in progress from the time it comes into being. I follow
its growth from beginning to publication and beyond. Students have become
very good editors of their own work because they accept peer review
willingly and spend much time reviewing their work and others. Oftentimes
I see students revise work months after publication.

The Internet provides an audience for my students: peers and mentors. Our students communicate with peers in Sweden, Japan, China, and Spain (http://199.233.193.1/ip.html), as well as with students around the United States. Our mentoring program (http://199.233.193.1/mentor/mentor.html) includes an Internet community which chooses to assist me in my classroom. We have had people from the business world, retirees, college students, and peers view our students' work and then comment on it. Essentially, people who choose to be mentors do it because they have decided to interact with students. Internet mentors do not come into the classroom, but instead visit virtually. They use e-mail to communicate and provide guidance, writing help, and an audience for my young writers.

I have always been a person who learned things by doing. I was told by sages that homework was practice, and everyone practiced. If I practiced throwing a ball, riding a bike, or playing the piano, then I should do my homework, they told me. When I became a sage, I dispensed the same axioms I had heard. My students practiced writing by writing. Now my students create, design, and publish their work on the Internet. They are learning about writing by writing and publishing. Publishing one's writing, after all, is one of the goals of writing, though it is often a forgotten part of the writing process. The World Wide Web changes all of that as young writers learn how to write by including publishing. Today learning by doing is called constructivism. Looking for a better way to teach writing has been a professional goal of mine since before I became a teacher. It has taken me over twenty years to realize a better way on the Internet, but I have realized a few things:

- Make sure each student has access to his or her own computer.
- Have each student create a homepage which provides immediate involvement and a sense of belonging.
- Provide multiple projects so the student can move from one project to another at will.
- Don't worry about providing all resources; leave some discoveries for the students.
- Work with the students, discover alongside them, show them how to follow hunches and clues to discovery.
- Keep it simple. Avoid glitzy, gourmet-type software.
- Use real-time applications as opposed to hypothetical situations.

- Look at what other teachers have done by examining their syllabi (http://199.233.193.1/resource.html#syl) and borrow ideas.
- Be willing to share ideas with others. Do not go it alone.

I began using computers in my writing classroom in 1983. Now with the Internet, I believe I have come to as perfect an environment for the student writer as possible. The Internet has eliminated many of the negative aspects of writing while providing many positive aspects. Write on!

3 Surfing the Net: Getting Middle School Students Excited about Research and Writing

Jean Boreen

I walked around the lab, noting how industrious my eighth graders looked as they slouched over their computer keyboards and "hunt-and-pecked" their way through the second draft of their first computer-generated paper of the year. They were doing exactly what I had asked them to do: use the computer to compose and revise a "how-to" paper. They had peer-conferenced and provided thoughtful suggestions to each other on how to make the papers better. But as I moved from student to student, I was still troubled by one thing: they didn't seem excited about using computers for their writing task.

Not that I expected them to be thrilled and turn somersaults whenever I mentioned that they would be allowed in the computer lab. But I had read articles that suggested that computers sparked more creative work from students, that they encouraged students to take greater chances with revision and their writing in general (Lucking and Stallard 1988; Selfe, Rodrigues, and Oates 1989; Standiford, Jaycox, and Auten 1983). So where was the excitement? The intrinsic motivation? And what would happen when the novelty of working on the computers passed? What was I doing wrong?

As time passed, I realized that I really wasn't doing anything *wrong*. But let's be realistic. Why is sitting in front of a computer doing word processing necessarily more interesting than sitting down with a sheet of paper and writing down one's thoughts in a logical manner? For many students, it's not.

Reprinted from Chapter 6 of *Weaving a Virtual Web*, edited by Sibylle Gruber.

I realized that I needed to find ways to enhance the computer work I was asking my students to complete.

"Surfing the Net: A Writing Workshop for Kids"

I now teach at the university level in an English Education program and consider it one of my responsibilities to prepare students for using technology to teach the writing process. Consequently, I developed a course called "Surfing the Net: A Writing Workshop for Kids" with the intent that it would provide concrete ideas for teachers on how to make computer work in the classroom more meaningful for secondary students. Offered during one of our five-week summer sessions, the course provides university students as well as veteran teachers with an opportunity to work one-on-one with a group of middle school—fourth through ninth grade—students in a computer-mediated classroom. Middle school students (who attend class the middle three weeks of the five-week session) have the chance to spend one week researching topics off the Internet before turning their attention to the various stages of the writing process. And adult students can experiment with how computer technology can be used to motivate and encourage enthusiasm in students as they work through the writing process.[1]

In this paper, I describe how the members of the class—middle school students, university students, veteran middle school teachers, university instructors—constructed and reconstructed various aspects of the course in order to meet the needs of all involved. Through this sharing of ideas and approaches, I hope to give classroom teachers more options when it comes to creative uses of technology in the classroom.

Challenging the Potential of Computers

We all work to make the writing *process* routine for students; the real challenge for teachers who have access to computer technology may be how to keep their students interested. Using the Internet as a research tool can be one of the most effective ways not only to heighten student enthusiasm for computer use itself but also as a way to influence how students explore and conceptualize what they want to accomplish with their writing. The exploratory nature of the Web is addressed by Heba (1997) who notes that "the experience of multimedia is more chaotic and, perhaps, appeals more to a rhetoric of exploration where the boundaries and destinations of the discourse are not always clear"(22). Students, from this perspective, can become engaged in a multitude of rhetorical activities without being restrained by a closely defined concept of "writing."

Connecting Computer Technology with Rhetorical Choices

One of the issues we dealt with in our "Surfing the Net" course was how to integrate process writing with computer technology in a manner that seemed natural and interesting to the middle school students. While a number of books and articles (Cotton 1996; Hawisher and LeBlanc 1992; LaQuey 1993; Merseth 1991; Reinhardt 1995; Sheingold and Hadley 1990) discussed the theoretical and pedagogical aspects of using computer technology in the classroom, it was not until the university students read texts like Nancie Atwell's *In the Middle* (1986) and Regie Routman's *Invitations: Changing as Teachers and Learners K–12* (1994) that they were able to conceptualize how to develop classroom writing and thinking strategies offered by this union of writing and technology.

Research Using the Internet

When I first taught this course in the summer of 1996, the offerings on the Internet were only adequate at best. For every site we found, there were typically two that we couldn't access or that simply didn't exist anymore. One year later, a search for information on "writing," for example, would give us anywhere from 50,000 to 1.2 million sites depending on the search engine— Lycos, Yahoo, Excite, Infoseek—chosen. So what do we as teachers do with this wealth of information as we plan instruction for and with our students? And how do we best prepare ourselves to work on this vast information highway?

Preparing the University Students

Many of the university students had never "surfed the Net" and were unclear as to what is offered on the World Wide Web. To give them a basic education on the use of Internet technology, our technology instructor, Fred Ducat, previewed for the university students much of the work they would be doing with the middle school students. For example, the students were instructed how to direct a "Key Search" on, as noted earlier, writing. The varied number of sites produced by the searches, based on the different search engines, exemplified for the university students just how much was available on the Web and how difficult it might be for their students to handle the huge amount of information and sites available. After all, when one has 50,000 sites to choose from and only a limited time to consider a small number of those, it is important to consider how these choices may affect individual students' creative processes.

Preparing the Middle School Students

One of the most motivational ways to help students become familiar with the World Wide Web is to ask them to go on an Internet treasure hunt. Working in pairs (or groups of four if one has a large class and few computers), students hunt out different sites and then look for specific information found on the site (see Figure 1).

This search technique is an excellent way for students to become acquainted with a variety of sites that may be of interest to them as they begin their own topic research. As this "hunt" list illustrates, students were asked to look for famous people, animals, authors, etc. Student comfort level with the Internet increases significantly as students become very adept at initiating key searches, typing in addresses, and quickly scanning for information. Once familiarity with the Net is established, students are more than ready for the next step: beginning the research for their writing project.

"I Want to Write a Mystery": Using the Internet for Source Material

When I asked my middle school students to "do research," I expected them to find information on specific topics and incorporate what they had found into short I-Search papers (Macrorie 1988) or persuasive essays. In giving these assignments, I hoped that students would take their facts, descriptions, and statistics and develop compositions that showed an understanding both of format and of the rhetorical choices possible when writing these types of essays.

During "Surf the Net," we found that using the Internet as a research tool could offer students additional ways to approach writing, especially in how the middle school students considered their rhetorical choices. Specifically, a student might begin research on a topic, a situation, or a place with the intent of writing one type of paper—informational essay, short story—and change her mind because of the wealth of options provided by the sheer volume of information found during prewriting.

Debbie loved mysteries. She also knew exactly what she wanted to accomplish during her three weeks: write a mystery in short story form. What she didn't have figured out were the specific details connected to the

Scavenger Hunt

The object of this scavenger hunt is to allow you to become more comfortable with the Internet and to see how it works. By the end of this hunt, you should have a better sense about the Net and what it can do.

Let's begin!

1. Find **Net Search** and click.
2. Choose **Info Seek** and click.
3. Choose the **Kids and Fun** selection and click.
4. Select **Silly Jokes**.
5. Scroll down the page until you can find **Kaitlyn's knock-knock jokes and riddles**.
6. Once you are at Kaitlyn's page, choose either **Knock-knock jokes or Riddles** at the middle of the page.
7. Now feel free to look at the whole site. Also, write down your favorite joke or riddle you find at this site.
8. Once you are done, click on the picture of **the house** at the top of the screen. Doing this will bring you back to where you started.
9. Now you should be back where we started.
10. Select **Net Search**.
11. Choose **Excite** this time.
12. Choose **Entertainment**.
13. Find and choose **Cartoons (editor's review)**.
14. Choose **Peanuts—The dog house** under today's cartoons.
15. Read the comic strip and then choose **Sunday Strip**.
16. Read the comic strip and go ahead and view other strips by selecting any date in the box at the bottom of the page. Write down the date of your favorite strip.
17. Once you are done, select the **Home (picture of the house)** key.
18. Here we go on another search. Choose **Net Search**.
19. Choose **Yahoo**.
20. Choose **Games**.
21. Choose **Puzzles**.
22. Choose **Tic Tac Toe**.
23. Choose **Steve's Tic Tac Toe**.
24. Play a few games to see if you can beat Steve. To play your "O", just click on the space where you would like to place it.
25. Once you are done, select the **Home key** and prepare to take one more journey on the Net.
26. Now we are going to try something different. At the top of the screen by the home key is a long box and the word **location**. There is an address already there but we are going to put our own address in the box. Take the mouse and place the cursor after location and click. You should see a blinking line. Now type in the address http://www.blacktop.com/coralforest.
27. After a few minutes, you should be at the coral reef. Go through this site and explore and find all of the different features this site has. Also, look at all the pictures of the sea. After you are done exploring, write down your favorite picture or your favorite place you visited on this site.
28. Choose the Home key. Congratulations! You have successfully completed the hunt!

Hunt created by Heather Nebrich and Ali Henderson

Figure 1. Internet Scavenger Hunt

plot machinations she had in mind. Debbie began with a Net search on Carlsbad, California, a place she had once been on vacation. As she and her university teacher, Mark, scanned sites, they found a picture of a flower field with a windmill in the middle of it. Debbie decided that this was where the main action of the plot would be. From there, she pulled up the "America's Most Wanted" site and looked for the kind of face she wanted her murderer to have; this sight proved too intriguing, though, as Debbie and Mark spent two full days reading the background blurbs on each case pulled from the site. As Debbie's experience shows, students can get bogged down easily and become frustrated while surfing the Web. A possible solution to circumvent information overload is to ask students to step back from their research and reconsider their writing strategies based on the data gathered. In our example, Debbie reconsidered and decided to re-outline the action of her story. Instead of packing the first chapter with physical characteristics of the protagonists and antagonists, she created a more action-filled beginning and let the characters show more of themselves through their interactions. Then, using the Internet information she had found, she began to contemplate how later chapters might look.

The Novelty of Interactive Sites, or "Meet the Spice Girls!"

Interactive sites have the potential to be highly motivational for younger students who are visual learners. Much like the educational games developed for younger children, interactive Web sites can present—with sound, pictures, and voice-overs—how a scientific concept like the bonding of molecules was conceived and then illustrate how the individual molecules are drawn together, how they bond, and what the resulting molecular structure might look like (http://www.nyu.edu/pages/mathmol/). The possibilities of what may be seen and heard on interactive sites is only limited to the imagination of the person who developed the site.

Allan bounced—literally—into class on the first day; we should have suspected then that he would be a student who would look for a high-energy topic to research and write about. Allan was an ardent "hip-hop" fan, and the English band the Spice Girls was one of his favorite groups. The first site Allan found as he and his teacher, Samantha, looked for information about the band was an informational site that had a picture of the five band members and a short bio on each one. Allan dutifully book marked the page but clearly was less than thrilled at what he had found. On his second try, a blast of music took the entire lab by surprise. The slightly glazed look in

Allan's eyes was replaced by an excited gleam as other students rushed over to see what he had found. On the screen, the Spice Girls danced as their mouths moved almost in sync with the music coming from the computer's speaker (http://www.serveyou.com/spice/songs.html). From that moment on, Allan was hooked, and he spent the rest of research week looking for similar exciting sites. One cautionary note: Samantha found out very quickly that if she let him, Allan would simply bounce from site to site unless something unique caught his attention. What teachers can do to avoid indiscriminate surfing is to make students read the information on each site thoroughly, then jot down a few notes or bookmark sites that had a great deal of information. In this way, students have to consider each site not only for its entertainment value, but also for its informational worth. This type of evaluation lends itself to the kind of critical thinking we want all of our students to embrace. Students need to read, evaluate, and choose information based on an understanding of why certain facts or ideas are more important within a specific assignment or in their search for enlightenment on a topic.

Conversation Anyone? E-mail and the Adolescent Researcher

For many of us, e-mail has become the correspondence of choice because of the speed and efficiency of the interchange. Like the use of personal interviews when students are creating I-Search papers, e-mail conversations allow questions and answers to move between interviewer and interviewee at a fairly rapid pace. However, we found that e-mail correspondence could offer additional rhetorical options that we hadn't even considered.

Amanda and her teacher Jody were having a hard time deciding which topic to choose for Amanda's writing project. Amanda's attitude about the topics she was researching reminded me of the old Lays' potato chips commercial—"You can't choose (eat) just one!" Shortly after her group decided that they wanted to put their writing in a newspaper format, Amanda found an interactive Web site on Edgar Allan Poe that included an obituary and a picture of the author's grave in Baltimore. This was Amanda's epiphany. "I'm going to create celebrity obituaries," she announced to her group.

Amanda decided that she would conduct searches on three or four of her favorite (living) authors. In the middle of her search on Danielle Steele, she realized that not one of the sites she had accessed listed Steele's age, a necessary ingredient in a successful obituary. As I listened to Amanda's plight, I noted that the site she had just pulled up listed an e-mail address for the author. At my suggestion, Amanda wrote to Steele, explaining the project, asking for her age ("Please be honest," Amanda wrote) and any other information Steele might want to offer about being a writer. Days passed without a response. Amanda became irritated with Steele and decided that the author would come to a "darker" end than she had originally intended: she would have her murdered by an unknown person, maybe a disgruntled reader.

As Amanda worked on the obituary, she became so intrigued with the mystery she was creating around the author's death that she decided to create a link between all of the obituaries. In a series of mysterious accidents, Steele, Beverly Cleary, and Stephen King all came to unusual ends, victims of Raymond, the "serial author" killer.

As this example shows, e-mail correspondence can create new venues for the middle school student. Whether authors write back or not, students can use their e-mail experiences to reconceptualize their writing task. Amanda might have been content to write the simple obituaries; however, her creative juices pushed her to write an article more intriguing and inventive. Furthermore, in order to make her piece more interesting, she had to look at police logs in newspapers and decide how to recreate the same tone.

Creating a Homepage: Yes, Middle School Students CAN Do This!

One of the adult student groups decided that they would like to help their students create a homepage as part of their group writing project. Middle school teacher Logan Bennett, "the female version of Bill Gates"(according to a classmate), convinced me and her teammates that the research and process writing that were part of the class objectives could naturally lead to Web page development. Because of my own experiences putting together a homepage, I was willing to let Logan and her team (Lee and Whitman) help the students develop sites as long as they didn't scrimp on the writing and research aspects of the course. They decided to divide the workload among groups of students: Lee handled the research and informational writing, Whitman worked on the creative writing aspect of the class, and Logan taught the students how to use html, find clip-art, use Adobe Photoshop and Graphic Converter, and so on. The adult teachers' hope was that the opportunity to work on a homepage would increase student motivation and encourage a greater willingness to hone skills related to the production of written work that would appear on the Internet.

Like the other groups, the homepage team and their students began by prowling around the Internet looking for sites that excited their imagination. As they surfed, they looked not only for interesting topics but also for innovative sites or clip art they found interesting. Moving from teacher to teacher, the students alternately took turns producing their creative work (a poem on Edgar Allan Poe or a song), detailing the information they wanted to use on their individual Web pages and fashioning the Web page itself. While the students were willing to make the creative effort, it was the Web page that caught and kept their attention. Similar to the writing process, Web page design needs to progress through various stages: students need to search for an interesting topic, decide on a specific topic, work on planning the Web page (text, background, graphics, etc.) and publish their information (upload to the Web). In the case of the students involved in this class, personal interests in Edgar Allan Poe, snowboarding, and bass guitar players became dynamic representations of the interests of each student. To access the student pages, go to

- http://www.nau.edu/~jmb5/initial/students/lucky/edgar.html
- http://www.nau.edu/~jmb5/initial/students/ryan/ryan'swebpage.html
- http://www.nau.edu/~jmb5/initial/students/wes/goodpage.html

Publishing on the Computer

Publishing student work, in many cases, increases students' enthusiasm for the task at hand. For this course, publishing took the form of a student booklet that would be shared with the other members of the class and their families and friends on the last meeting day for the middle school students. And, of course, we had the Web pages our three students put together. In this sense, the computers offered us another use, a different outlet for student creativity that went beyond the simple word processing aspect most of us take for granted. In case students do not have their own Web site, the Internet offers a number of sites that allow students to put their work online and receive feedback from others who also choose to access these publishing sites:

- KidPub: http://www.kidpub.org/kidpub
- Book Nook: http://www.i-site.on.ca/booknook.html
- Ace Kids: http://www.acekids.com/bkground.html

Final Reflections

In this final section, I would like to consider what conclusions we can draw for teachers who are trying to integrate the writing process and technology in their own classrooms.

Wedding Writing and Technology

As most of my students realized fairly quickly, this joining of approaches is not always the easiest to accomplish. As Lee noted toward the end of the first week with the students,

> We took the kids down the hall to talk about each other's progress. This was supposed to be the time where the three of us talked to the students about how they were coming along with their projects, and it ended up being a time where we spouted off our ideas for the individual deadlines for their work. I was interested in the structure they would develop for the research part of the project, Whitman was concerned as to the ideas they planned to use for the creative aspects of their writing, and Logan wanted to know what they wanted to use from their research and creative work on their Web pages. We were acting like the three activities were mutually exclusive.

Once they realized the interconnectivity of these activities, however, using the Internet became integral to the writing process.

Impacting the Stages of the Writing Process

The addition of the Internet component for research adds possibilities and frustrations to the prewriting and drafting stages of the process. The potential for motivating excitement about conducting research is enormous with the Internet because of the immediacy and variety of the information. As Leah, one of the adult students, noted,

> I saw this [class] as an opportunity to spend quality time with a student teaching useful information that he would be able to utilize the rest of his days. Sam [the student] was a joy to be around. He needed little instruction to be off and running with this writing project. As a matter of fact, I found it difficult to let him work independently. It is always a goal of mine to get my students to claim personal responsibility for their education, but I found in this situation how difficult it was to keep my hands off and let him write. I felt that I should be actively participating in his education. But then I realized that I could model time spent reading and writing for him even as he was spreading his wings with his own story telling/writing.

Leah, in this excerpt, is aware of the added dimensions created by using the Internet as a research tool. However, once she realizes the importance of letting her student explore his own writing process, she is able to modify her own "traditional" teaching behavior.

Using Student Ease with Technology to Extend Educational Parameters

Many students who have grown up with computers in their homes and classrooms easily embrace their computer work. They have little fear of the technology itself and often find it easier to "pull" information from the Net than from card catalogs or the *Reader's Guide to Periodical Literature*. Our middle school students found that the Internet made much of the information they needed more accessible. And they were able to use the time they may have "saved" to think about how the data they had found could be incorporated into their writing.

Creating New Experts: Letting Students Take Charge of Their Own Education

In addition, the use of the Internet in the classroom becomes a learning experience for teachers, especially in the way they can allow their students to become experts. Logan noted two things about her experience with Web page development. First, Wes, who created "Wes' Hippy Juicer Web Page," was so "into" Web pages that he eventually surpassed Logan's knowledge of Web development. Wes then began helping his classmates, as well as other adults in the class, with their Web site preparation. Second, for herself as teacher, Logan commented that

> I was extremely proud of the kids and myself as I had never taught Web page design before. I like the idea that one can do something active, actually create from scratch a *working* piece of writing you might say. I am glad you gave us the freedom to push that envelope and expand the writing process in the area of design. I now know that I can teach students to make a working page from scratch and get up on the Net.

Integrating Web-based research skills can promote student and teacher learning if we are willing to allow for new and innovative approaches to teaching with and about the Web. Most school districts have noted the importance of student fluency with technology, so teachers will need to continue to look for opportunities to connect computer technology with the everyday aspects of student education. Using the Internet as a research tool may be one fairly time-efficient way of accomplishing this goal.

Note

1. For many reasons, this course attempted to accomplish more in three weeks than most of us would in ordinary teaching situations. The middle school students were with us for one hour and fifteen minutes for twelve days, and one of those was devoted to the publishing party we held during our final meeting with them. That meant that our young authors had to prewrite, research, draft, peer conference, revise, and edit in only eleven days. And while many of the adult students had taken a mini-institute on the writing process and how to teach it effectively through the Northern Arizona Writing Project, there were some who had little experience teaching writing but were curious about using the Internet in a research capacity. In addition, the university students worked within three- to four-person teaching units as they planned daily and weekly lessons for their particular middle school students based on the various writing projects the groups decided to create. Combined with this was the reality of how challenging computer technology can be, especially in lab settings.

Works Cited

Atwell, Nancie. 1984. *In the Middle: Writing, Reading, and Learning with Adolescents*. Portsmouth, NH: Boynton/Cook-Heinemann.

Cohen, M., and M. Reil. 1986. *Computer Networks: Creating Real Audiences for Students' Writing*. Technical Report No. 15. San Diego, CA: Interactive Technology Laboratory, University of California.

Cotton, Eileen. 1996. *The Online Classroom: Teaching with the Internet*. Bloomington, IN: ERIC Edinfo Press.

Hawisher, Gail, and Paul LeBlanc, eds. 1992. *Re-Imagining Computers and Composition: Teaching and Research in the Virtual Age*. Portsmouth, NH: Boynton/Cook-Heinemann.

Heba, Gary. 1997. "HyperRhetoric: Multimedia, Literacy, and the Future of Composition." *Computers and Composition* 14(1): 19–44.

International Association for the Evaluation of Educational Achievement. *Computers in American Schools*, 1992. Minneapolis, MN: USA IEA. http://www.socsci.umn.edu/%7Eia

LaQuey, T. 1993. *Internet Companion*. New York: Addison-Wesley.

Lucking, R., and C. Stallard. 1988. *How Computers Can Help You Teach English*. Portland, ME: J. Weston Walch.

Macrorie, Ken. 1988. *The I-Search Paper*. Portsmouth, NH: Boynton/Cook.

Merseth, K. 1991. "Supporting Beginning Teachers with Computer Networks. *Journal of Teacher Education* 42(2): 140–47.

Mike, D. 1996. "Internet in the Schools: A Literacy Perspective." *Journal of Adolescent and Adult Literacy* 40: 14–21.

Reinhardt, A. 1995. "New Ways to Learn." *BYTE* (March): 50–71.

Rogers, A. 1992. *Linking Teachers and Students around the World*. Bonita, CA: FrEdMail Foundation.

Routman, Regie. 1994. *Invitations: Changing as Teachers and Learners K–12*. Portsmouth, NH: Heinemann.

Selfe, Cynthia L., Dawn Rodrigues, and William R. Oates, eds. 1989. *Computers in English and the Language Arts: The Challenge of Teacher Education*. Urbana, IL: National Council of Teachers of English.

Sheingold, K., and M. Hadley. 1990. *Accomplished Teachers: Integrating Computers into Classroom Practice*. Special Report. New York: Center for Technology in Education.

Standiford, Sally N., Kathleen Jaycox, and Anne Auten. 1983. *Computers in the English Classroom: A Primer for Teachers*. Urbana: ERIC Clearinghouse on Reading and Communication Skills and the National Council of Teachers of English.

4 Oh, What a Tangled Web We've Woven! Helping Students Evaluate Sources

Susan A. Gardner, Hiltraut H. Benham, and
Bridget M. Newell

Writing research papers before the advent of the personal computer and the growth of the Internet was not at all like the task faced by high school and college students today. Doing research in *the olden days* was an endless and well-defined process for English teachers. As students, we started by choosing a topic, narrowing it, and then trying to create a thesis sentence to guide the research. Then came the research, introduced by a mandatory library tour complete with instructions on using the card catalog, reference books, and *Readers' Guide to Periodical Literature.* Once we actually began searching for resources, we hoped nobody had checked out those sources we needed. Endless hours of reading and transferring information onto note cards often preceded any real thinking or writing about the topic.

Later, as we became those English teachers assigning research papers, we realized we needed to instruct students in the same laborious research process: Make notes on index cards; make a bibliography card for each source; key every note card to source and type. Explaining the type of note card meant we had to teach students the differences among a direct quote, precis, paraphrase, and summary. Bibliographic format, of course, filled several more hours, as we drilled the students in proper placement of commas, dates, and underlining in MLA style. Then, once our students had mastered these techniques and accumulated enough note and bibliography

Reprinted from *English Journal*, September 1999.

cards, they would be ready to write a coherent, captivating research paper. Or so we told ourselves.

Enter the Internet

In high schools and colleges today, English teachers and their colleagues across the curriculum are still assigning research papers. Students still go through a process to research and locate suitable sources for their topics, but the personal computer and access to the vast and tangled web of the Internet have revolutionized the research paper assignment. Not only does word processing, with its quick and easy revision applications, make writing the paper easier, the ability to find resources via the Web makes researching appealing, almost glitzy, to adolescents. Teens enjoy the electronic medium for research; having to surf the Web looking for sources is almost a forced pleasure. They are attracted by the graphics and multimedia extras; they find jumping from link to link in nano-seconds more enjoyable than paging through indexes of thick books. For these students, scanning screens is not as miserable as reading lengthy hard copy articles.

Teachers everywhere, of course, are alarmed by the new technology and what it is doing to writing and research. In a recent *New York Times* article, Steven Knowlton suggests that "without guidance, the Internet's wealth of data can lead to poor research papers" (18). A few months before, David Rothenberg noted the same problem in his article, "How the Web Destroys the Quality of Students' Research Papers." A *Salt Lake Tribune* article, "Is Internet Cheat Sheet or Tool for Education?" describes sites that offer papers for sale, while surveying English teachers' opinions on the use of the Internet to teach writing.

Of course, the more we use the Internet, the more we know both its capabilities and its pitfalls as an educational tool. Points we all recognize, however, are that the Internet is here to stay, it will be used for research, and we can't ignore its power for engaging our students in writing the traditional term paper.

The Problem of Sources

The problem of sources really isn't a new one, nor one linked exclusively to Web sites. Published guides such as James D. Lester's *Writing Research*

Papers always contain a section on evaluating sources. Standard procedure in teaching the research process to students is to lecture on source quality and credibility. Teachers generally talk about how to know if the book a student has located is a good one for information as well as a credible resource intellectually. We're not sure students always listen. We still receive papers in which students use popular periodicals such as *Good Housekeeping, Family Circle,* and *Redbook* as authoritative sources of knowledge instead of academic journals. To many students, a source—any source—on the topic is just that, a source. They mostly want to find the required number of sources to flesh out their bibliographies and to have enough information to piece together, in patchwork fashion, the required number of pages for their research paper assignment.

Helping students learn to navigate and evaluate the staggering amount of information on the Web may actually prove a blessing for English teachers. We have found it so. When we take students to the lab and walk them through the important features of a credible Web site, we have found that, *finally*, they start applying the same criteria to print sources—something we thought we had been teaching prior to the use of electronic research. We end up discussing what makes a viable print source as often as we explain the qualities that make a good Web source.

Unfortunately, students don't always understand what they see on their monitors when they are surfing the Internet. First, they do not know how to differentiate between electronic library resources and public Internet sites. For example, they may assume that a database posted on the Web is as reliable as personal pages that are also published on the Web. In reality, electronic databases are posted by publishers who screen the content and then organize the resources. Second, students do not realize that Web pages generally do not adhere to any criteria before they can be posted to the Internet. Librarians assure that quality materials are placed in the library, but on the Web anyone can publish a home page. No one entity screens and organizes pages published on the Web.

Evaluating Web Resources

Because of the immensity of information—worthwhile and not so worthwhile—on the Web and because of the confusion over all the electronic resources posted on it, we really do need to teach our students how to evaluate what's out there. One of the first steps is to explain the extension domains. The domain provides information about the authority and perhaps even the bias of the source. For example, sometimes students may want to find information from a *.com* site for a paper, but they should know that such a site *is* commercial and has something to sell. Following is the current list of top level domains on the Internet:

.com	commercial entity
.edu	educational institution
.gov	government agency or department
.mil	military organization
.net	network resource
.org	other type of organization, usually not-for-profit
.firm	businesses
.store	online stores
.web	Web related organizations
.arts	cultural and entertainment organizations
.rec	organizations emphasizing recreational activities
.info	organizations that provide information
.nom	individuals who want to be identified as such

With the interest in having students publish their papers on the Web, often as a class project, perhaps another domain ought to be created. A domain of *.stu* would let surfers know that this information is from a student writer's work and not from a psychologist, a sociologist, or other credentialed source. Too often students don't realize the source they've decided to quote is another student paper.

What are the important criteria, then, for establishing the credibility of a Web resource? These criteria are identical, for the most part, to what we use to measure the quality of a print resource: authorship, accuracy, objectivity, currency, and coverage.

Authority

James Strickland notes in *From Disk to Hard Copy:*

> . . . there's no way to tell who is or is not an authority on the Net. To author tends to give one authority . . . In cyberspace, anyone can claim authority, posing as one who knows things, presenting

> information in a format identical to those whom others would consider experts." (90)

The authorship of a Web site is often difficult to determine. Many times the list of qualifications is absent, and there is no link available to a home page. On the Web, the home page is the sponsor, similar to a publisher in the traditional setting.

When students are trying to establish the authorship and affiliation of a Web page, they should consider the following questions:

- Is the author's name listed?
- What are the author's credentials? Do these identify the author as an authority in the field?
- Is the author's institutional affiliation listed and linked to the home page of that institution?
- Is the relationship between the institution and the author clear?
- Does the author list an address (e-mail or snail mail) or phone number for contact?
- Is there a link to the author's biographical information?

A well-constructed, credible Web site will have many of these informational items present. If they are missing, students should beware.

Accuracy

In addition to being able to investigate information about the author, students will want to be able to evaluate the accuracy of the information or claims presented on the Web site. Again, they need to remember that *anyone* can publish a Web page. At this point there are no standards and no type of control in place for pages published on the Web. Questions students will want to consider include the following:

- Is the information reliable and free from errors?
- Is a bibliography included to verify the information?
- Is it clear who is responsible for the accuracy of the material?
- Are there links to other reliable sources?
- If statistical material is included, are the sources for these materials clearly stated?

Objectivity

Students should know that Web pages seldom state the goal or aim of the author. Many times a Web page is only a sounding board for the author. Students will want to clearly differentiate advertisement from actual information on Web pages. To make this distinction, they should carefully look at the domain extension and ask the following questions:

- Is the information presented with the least possible bias?
- Is the site factual, or does the author try to change the user's mind?
- Are graphics or imagery used to sway the opinion of the user?

Currency

One of the exciting features of the Web is the idea that the information is the most up-to-date, cutting-edge material available. Publishing to the Web is simple and fast and can be revised quickly as new findings occur. In comparison, publishing in print can take years. But just how current is information on the Web? Students need to be cautioned that not all pages contain dates, and dates given on Web pages can have various meanings. A date on a Web page can indicate when the information was actually written, when the page was put on the Web, or when the page was last revised. As students evaluate Web pages, they should ask the following questions:

- Is the date of the latest revision of the site clearly stated?
- Is the date given for when the information was gathered?
- Is the page kept current?
- Are the links current; i.e., do they really work?
- Is this truly the latest information on the topic?

The best site is the one that defines the meaning of the date. If no date is given on a Web site, however, teachers can help students access that information by sending them to the directory in which the site resides. To access the document directory, users should click on "view" in the menu bar, and then click on "pageinfo." The last modification date of the page should be listed there.

Coverage

Coverage is one of the slipperiest Web page areas to evaluate. It is difficult to determine the coverage of a Web site, especially for our students who may not be familiar with a research topic. Students need to be fairly familiar with what has been published in print to know if the site covers the topic in depth. Still, the following questions may help students analyze the coverage of a site:

- Is the scope of the topic clearly stated?
- Are supporting materials (bibliography, charts, statistics, graphics, etc.) given?
- Are there links to other resources on the topic?
- Is the site still under construction?

Web Sites on Evaluation

Although the five criteria we use will help teachers assist students in evaluating sources they find on the Web, several sites specifically focus on this process. One of the most thorough and comprehensive is Robert Harris's site, "Evaluating Internet Research Sources" at http://www.sccu.edu/faculty/R_Harris/ evalu8it.htm. Harris, who is affiliated with Southern California College, provides extensive background for teachers, almost a mini-course on Web site evaluation. Anything teachers or students might want to know about evaluation of Web sites can be found on this well-maintained site. Another helpful site dealing with evaluation is found at http://www.lib.lfc.edu/evalweb.html, published by the Library and Information Technology Staff of Lake Forest College. An important feature on this brief site is the inclusion of good and questionable examples for each criteria, which may make the evaluating of sites clearer for students. Finally, Kathy Schrock's "Critical Evaluation Information" page, which is located at http://discoveryschool.com/ schrockguide/eval.html, contains valuable links to other Web sites that discuss evaluating the quality and credibility of Web resources.

The Research Paper and Web Evaluation

Teachers who want students to incorporate Internet information in papers will want to set up their research assignments carefully. We've found that balancing the number and type of resources—electronic and hard copy—in our assignments works well. Initially, as we had students use Internet resources in their papers, we asked them to print out the pages they directly cited or used in their bibliography. These printouts were for the protection of both of us. Web sites can vanish from one day to the next, so having a printout established that the site really did exist. In addition, it was easy for us as teachers to check the source to see how accurately students used the material and how appropriate the wording was. We also felt that asking students to provide printouts of their electronic materials reduced plagiarism. Students determined to plagiarize could still find ways around this safeguard, but for many, being responsible for turning in their electronic research was a sufficient deterrent.

Even with a well-written handout on the research paper assignment, teachers will still want to guide students through some Web evaluation exercises. We found an outstanding activity that two University of Albany, SUNY, librarians—Trudi Jacobson and Laura Cohen—describe in *The Teaching Professor*. They ask students to do some site analysis on a Web site of their choice. Students ask four questions about the site:

- Who posted the information?
- What authority or special knowledge does the author have?
- Does the site show bias or slant?
- When was the site last revised?

After this first analysis, students go to a page the librarians have created for the assignment called "The Psychosocial Parameters of Internet Addiction." Working in pairs, students analyze information, which is supposed to be an authoritative, annotated bibliography on the topic written by a professor in a Department of "Psychotechnology." The librarians carefully guide discussion of the individual items and then ask students to click on the "additional information" link where they discover that the page is a fake. Jacobson and Cohen generously "invite others to take a look at and use the page" (4). The address is http://www.albany.edu/library/internet/addiction.html.

We adapted this assignment by bookmarking three distinctly different Web sites and having students compare the pages based on the criteria discussed in this article. We then send students to the bogus "Psychosocial" site to analyze what appears to be a wonderfully helpful bibliography posted on the Web. Done in close succession in one class period, this exercise is an eye-opening contrast for students.

Web Evaluation Assignments

Teachers will want to create their own Web evaluation assignments appropriate to their classes, students, and degree of access to the Internet, but we have used a variety of the following short assignments to help our students become Web savvy. These assignments can be used prior to assigning a research paper, or they can be used independent of a long project. The point of the activities is to make these criteria for evaluating Web sites "stick"; we find it very helpful to have students produce writing assignments that require them to apply evaluation criteria while also learning about a relevant topic. Three such assignments are a summary report, an annotated bibliography, and an evaluation report.

Summary Report

The goal of this assignment is to determine the extent to which a Web site is helpful for high school students wanting to use it as a resource in writing a research paper. The site might focus on a specific author or piece of literature, on the principles of writing, or on background information about a topic. Students choose one site and first use a checklist to determine factual information about the site. We have used the guide shown in Figure 1 with our students before having them write a short report.

Once they have examined the site carefully and completed the checklist, we have students write a brief report responding to three questions: What kind of information is presented in this site? Is the information credible? How is the site useful for high school students?

Annotated Bibliography

A productive second assignment is to have students identify a set number of Web sites that focus on a specific topic; e.g., *Of Mice and Men,* The World of Shakespeare, or the use of the comma. Then, depending on the teacher's goals and students' level of sophistication, we require students to annotate and present a summary of the site's content and credibility. This activity works well as a stand-alone project emphasizing research, analysis, and writing skills, but it could also be used to develop a class list of credible Web sites for students to use in their research projects.

Some criteria to look at before citing an Internet document in a bibliography:

Author

- What is the author's name? _____
- Are the author's credentials listed?   YES   NO
- Is the author's affiliation listed?   YES   NO
- Is there a link to the home page
  of the author's institution?   YES   NO
- Does the author provide a link
  to his/her biographical page?   YES   NO

Document Information

- List the date of the last
  revision of the document _____
- Does the document have a header
  or footer with site information?   YES   NO
- Can the information be verified
  with given references?   YES   NO
- If the document quotes statistics,
  can you tell if the statistics are
  from a reliable or credible source?   YES   NO
- Can the information be verified
  with given references?   YES   NO
- Can you contact the Webmaster
  from the document?   YES   NO
- Are the links to other
  documents working?   YES   NO

These items *must be present* in order
to give a site validity.

Figure 1. Internet Evaluation List.

Evaluation Report

An extension of the summary report, the evaluation report is a more challenging and in-depth exercise that works well with more advanced students. While the summary report requires students to look at factual information about one Web site, this project requires them to evaluate *how well* a site meets the five credibility criteria and *how well* it explains information to a high school student. The evaluation process goes into more depth and asks for a critical report that demonstrates a reflective examination of the site from the points of credibility, content, and presentation of information.

Of course, each of these assignments can be tailored to a particular class's needs and a teacher's pedagogical goals. Regardless of how the assignment is customized for a class, the value of these assignments is that they require students to *apply* lessons on Web site credibility while also developing their critical thinking and writing skills.

Final Thoughts

As we think of the research paper assignment today, we realize that much of the process remains the same as it did years ago. We still choose a topic, narrow it, create a thesis, and do research. What has changed are the tools we use. We now have technology to do much of the work for us, and although it is easier to find resources on the Internet, contrary to popular views, the selection of appropriate information has not been simplified with the use of the Web.

Teachers have an immense challenge in helping students develop a critical eye toward what they can access with a few keystrokes. The challenge goes far beyond the use of credible sources for research papers. Students now access the Net to find information on travel, recreation, health, the government, and so on. They will be using the Internet for life, and they need to be able to distinguish the genuine from the bogus on the sites they enter. Teaching students evaluation strategies is the critical element in research, for only with such strategies will our students be able to untangle the intricate Web we've woven.

Works Cited

Bryson, Robert. "Is Internet Cheat Sheet or Tool for Education." *The Salt Lake Tribune* 14 Sept. 1997: B1.

Jacobson, Trudi E., and Laura B. Cohen. "Teaching Students to Evaluate Internet Sites." *The Teaching Professor* Aug./Sept. 1997: 4.

Knowlton, Steven R. "How Students Get Lost in Cyberspace." *New York Times* 2 Nov. 1997, late ed., sec. 4a: 18+.

Lester, James D. *Writing Research Papers: A Complete Guide.* 8th ed. New York: HarperCollins, 1996.

Rothenberg, David. "How the Web Destroys the Quality of Students' Research Papers." *The Chronicle of Higher Education* 15 Aug. 1997: A44.

Strickland, James. *From Disk to Hard Copy: Teaching Writing with Computers.* Portsmouth, NH: Heinemann-Boynton/Cook, 1997.

5 Poetry and the Internet

Albert B. Somers

Any effort to describe the presence of poetry or any other topic on the sprawling Internet is rife with risk. The moment the ink dries—or the cursor blinks off—the news is old. Still, with almost every American school already online a book like this can hardly keep its head in the sand.

By now there's no need to explain what the Internet is. Even those who haven't jumped on board are well aware of its presence. We've all seen the cover stories in *Time* and *Newsweek* and the shelves of books in every library and bookstore (*The Internet for Dummies,* et al.). The yellow pages of even midsize city phone directories now have multiple listings under "Internet Services" (mine has twenty-nine). Web site addresses abound, and "www dot whatever dot com" has become one of the mantras of our age.

But surely poetry, some might wanly hope—this purest and gentlest of genres with its flashes of imagination and subtle layers of meaning—surely poetry has remained impervious to cyberspace. Not so. The Internet offers students and teachers of poetry a wealth of resources, among them files of information about poetry and poets, texts of poems (for the most part the classics, whose copyrights long ago expired, or the poems of "Wordsworth wannabes" anxious to offer their work online), and discussion groups of poets, teachers, and sometimes just readers and admirers of poetry. Even lesson plans for teaching poetry are available.

Also consider this: when I first began looking for Internet homepages on poetry in the spring of 1995, I found a few hundred. As of this writing (spring 1999), they number in the thousands, with many more to come.

For teachers there are many possible avenues of access. Some enter specific homepage addresses (URLs). Without them, the best device is a

---

Reprinted from Chapter 12 of *Teaching Poetry in High School* by Albert B. Somers.

"search engine" like Yahoo, Lycos, or Infoseek. Search engines allow the user to type in a word or phrase, like "haiku" or "Robert Frost." In a matter of seconds, the engine riffles through its thousands of Web sites in search of the word and generates a list of matching items. When I entered the all-encompassing *poetry*, I was given a hierarchy of subheadings:

Anthologies	Magazines
Awards	Organizations
Beat Generation	Performance
Children's	Poem of the Day
Commercial Books	Poem of the Week
Countries and Cultures	Poets
Events	Publishers
Haiku	Science Fiction, Fantasy, Horror
Humorous	Web published poetry
Journals	Writing

Clicking on one of the items (e.g., Events) led to an annotated list of homepages (e.g., The Asheville Poetry Festival). In this way, search engines guide the user down through the hierarchy until he finds something interesting.

The above columns of headings represent to some degree the kinds of Web sites devoted to poetry. Among the best of them are general, all-purpose sites that embrace almost every aspect of the genre.[1]

General Poetry Sites

Perhaps the best of these sites is *The Academy of American Poets* homepage (http://www.poetsociety.org/). This is a handsome, well-designed production. It includes a listening booth where you can hear over ninety contemporary poets reading their work, a calendar of online poetry events (e.g., Seamus Heaney reading at the 92nd Street Y in New York City on September 28, 1998), and a variety of exhibits useful to teachers (like thematic collections on Daughters, Poems of Grief, Poems of Love, and Poems of Ancestry). There is also a Find-a-Poet database and a clickable list of almost a hundred links to other sites. This is a tremendous resource.

Another general site well worth exploring is *Poetry Society of America* (http://www.bookwire.com/psa/psa.html). This page includes sections on a

Calendar of Events, Awards, an Online Peer Workshop (where poets can post poems and have them discussed), Resources, and Poetry in Motion, the program that places placards of poems on buses and subways in New York City, Atlanta, Portland, and other cities. Poetry in Motion has a feature enabling users to send a friend a beautifully illustrated e-mail Poetry Postcard.

Web Sites on Poets

Like all other categories, Web sites devoted to acclaimed poets are growing in number. Most of them are developed and maintained by individuals with university connections who have a particular fondness for a poet; some are not unlike fan clubs.

It is hard to imagine a more comprehensive and beautiful homepage on modern poets than *Twentieth-century Poetry in English* (http://www.lit.kobe-u.ac.jp/~hishika/20c_poet.htm). This is a Japanese Web site created and maintained by Michael Eiichi Kishikawa. It includes not only handsome pages on Auden, Eliot, Frost, Stevens, Williams, and several other modern giants, but hundreds of links to others.

More contemporary in its focus is *The Internet Poetry Archive* (http://sunsite.unc. edu/dykki/poetry/), a joint venture of the University of North Carolina and the North Carolina Arts Council. This site currently presents biographical information, poems (including audio files), a bibliography, and photographs of six poets—Seamus Heaney, Czeslaw Milosz, Philip Levine, Robert Pinsky, Margaret Walker, and Yusef Komunyakaa.

Even more restricted is *Cowboy Poets on the Internet* (http://www.westfolk.org/), a handsome homepage sponsored by the Western Folklife Center in Elko, Nevada. Sections include poems and songs, a brief history of cowboy poetry, an exhibit gallery, audio clips, and lists of recordings and books.

Increasingly, there are homepages on particular poets:

Emily Dickinson (http://www.planet.net/pkrisxle/emily/dickinson.html) includes links to 460 of her poems, a biography, pictures, access to a discussion list on the poet, even her recipe for Black Cake. There is also a list of FAQs (Frequently Asked Questions) about her.

Maya Angelou Pages (http://members.aol.com/bonvibre/mangelou.html) and the *Maya Angelou Home Page* (http://www.cwrl.utexas.edu/~mmaynard/

Maya/maya5.html) are both sites with pictures, a biography, and poems. The first is linked to sites on other poets.

Life at Eagle Pond: The Poetry of Jane Kenyon and Donald Hall (http://www.sc.library.unh.edu/specoll/exhibits/kenhall.htm) is a beautiful Web site that includes selected poems, twenty drafts of Hall's poem "Ox-Cart Man," and a tribute to Kenyon, who died of leukemia in 1995.

Web sites sponsored by acclaimed poets themselves are less common, but Marge Piercy has her own, the *Marge Piercy Homepage* (http://www.capecod.net/~tmpiercy/), which includes sections on resume and biography, new projects, bibliography, interviews, and criticism, as well as several poems. Carolyn Forché also has her own site—*Carolyn Forché* (http://osf1.gmu.edu/~cforchem/index.html).

Much of the Internet's magic, of course, is serendipitous. Often I've lucked into interesting collections of poems by virtually unknown poets. One worth perusing is *In the Pockets of the Night,* a small group of poems by Elizabeth Herron on exhibit at the Sonoma State University Web site in California (http://libweb.sonoma.edu/exhibits/EH/). Many high school students would like her "Lake Trout," "Song," "When I Kiss You," and "Migration."

Migration

If my words can be
as honest as desire
they will go to you

like a flow of caribou over ice.
They will lick the air
like a migration

of wild geese, spill
like salmon up
stream. Words of a primal

instinct, pulling us
into an urgent journey
knowing though we know not

where, we're going
home.

Another lucky find for me was *Karen Tellefsen* (http://www.interactive.net/~kat/karen. html). Tellefsen is a chemist who writes mostly poems that rhyme. She has posted some fifty of them on her own homepage, including this one:

Galatea

Her face is like a feather, but her skull is more a stone.
Her hair is coiled in dreadlocks that resist the sculptor's comb.
Stalagtite stoicism is bred deeper than the bone.
She rises very early, and she always sleeps alone.

Her skin is thin as plaster milk; her fragrance is of chalk
that scratches on a dusty slate. Her every morning walk
is briskly clipped and measured so she never stops to talk
of alabaster fountains rising in a fleshy stalk.

She models flesh of perfect form while posing on her block,
so stiff, she never winces while cosmetic chisels knock
her less than lovely bits away. A stone may only mock
the breath that shatters life, and she is marble, solid rock.

Unlike these, most of the Web sites of obscure poets are the creations of
beginners whose work is anything but polished. For them, the Internet has
become an enormous vanity press. There are hundreds of them, and while
all of them deserve respect, most are quite forgettable and best left
unexplored.

Collections of Poetry

The Internet is fast becoming an enormous collection of poetry written
mostly by dead poets whose copyright privileges have also long since
expired. Check out *Project Bartleby Archive* (http://www.columbia.edu/
acis/bartleby), where you will find hundreds of poems by the likes of
Dickinson, Eliot, Frost (over a hundred poems), Hardy, Hopkins, Housman,
Millay, Sandburg, Sassoon, Whitman, and Yeats.

The *CMU Poetry Index of Canonical Verse* (http://eng.hss.cmu.edu/
poetry/) sounds impressive and is. Like *Project Bartleby*, it has complete texts
of many poems by mostly deceased poets (Browning, Byron, Marvell,
Spenser, Whitman, etc.), but also a few by moderns like Angelou, Auden,
cummings, Housman, Millay, and Pound.

Even better is *Poetry Daily* (http://www.poems.com/), which features a
new poem every day by a contemporary poet—it was "Aurelia Aurita" by
Regina O'Melveny the last day I looked—as well as a huge archive of all the
poems shown in the past, almost three hundred as of May 1998. *Poetry
Daily* also has a wonderful News and Features section.

The Writer's Almanac (http://almanac.mpr.org) is the Web site for Garrison
Keillor's daily five-minute radio program of the same name featured on many

public stations. Keillor ends each program with a poem, many of which are included in the Web site's Archives. The site also links to numerous others about poets and poetry.

Poetry Magazines and Journals

Established magazines are devoting Web sites to poetry. Among the best is the online version of *Poets & Writers Magazine* (http://www.pw.org), a cornucopia of goodies, including access to *P & W*'s catalog, a directory of addresses of poets and writers, suggestions on publishing, access to online conversations about poetry, and "News from the Writing World." Also worth a look is *Atlantic Unbound: Poetry Pages* (http://www.theatlantic.com/atlantic/atlweb/poetry/poetpage.htm), a Web site of *The Atlantic Monthly* with articles, poems published in the magazine, and "an Audible Anthology" of dozens of contemporary poets reading their own work.

Just as there are dozens of "little magazines" throughout the country devoted to poetry, there are many online journals ("webzines") embracing the same cause. Many have gaudy names—*Breakfast Surreal, Green Bison Quarterly, Headless Buddha*, and *Angel Exhaust*. A few are as conventional as their printed counterparts, but many push the envelope: *Forklift, Ohio* describes itself as a journal "of poetry, cooking, and light industrial safety." The quality of the poetry in most of these Web sites is spotty at best, but some of them may surprise. Four worth exploring are *Switched-on Gutenberg* (http://weber.u.washington. edu/~jnh/), *web del sol* (http://www.webdelsol.com/), *CrossConnect* (http://tech1.dccs.upenn.edu/~xconnect/) and the *Quarterly Review of Literature Poetry Series* (http://www.princeton.edu/~qrl/poetryseries.html).

In the future, established literary magazines will surely develop their own Web sites, following the lead of *Ploughshares* (http://www.emerson.edu/ploughshares/Ploughshares.html), the esteemed little magazine that has been publishing quality poetry and fiction since 1971. A journal aimed at young adults with its own Web site is *Writes of Passage* (http://www.writes.org/).

Web Sites on Writing Poetry

A classic homepage on writing poetry is The *Shiki Internet Haiku Salon* (http://mikan.cc.matsuyama-u.ac.jp:80/~shiki/). *Shiki* is a fascinating Japan-based site that introduces the familiar three-line poem. It includes a wonderful lesson plan for teaching the form and opportunities for users to add their own haiku to the collection in the database. A related site is *The Bi-weekly Kukai Report* (http://mikan.cc.matsuyama-u.ac.jp:80/~shiki/kukai.html), which offers a judged competition. Participants are invited to submit haiku on an identified "season word" (e.g., *beach* or *autumn wind*) and await the results.

On the other end of the continuum, perhaps, is *Poetry [a click and drag diversion]* (http://www.prominence.com/java/poetry/). Using Java technology and inspired by the Magnetic Poetry Kit available in bookstores, this clever Web site gives users dozens of word tabs for dragging around the screen to create a poem. It's great fun!

The Albany Poetry Workshop (http://www.sonic.net/poetry/albany/) offers "an interactive forum for poets and writers." Opportunities include on-going group poems, writing exercises, and feedback sessions for submitted poems.

Lesson Plans and Class Projects

Cyberspace is loaded with lesson plans although most seem to be written for elementary school math and science teachers. Still, there are sites with plans for teaching high school poetry as well, like *The Poetry Page* (http://www3.sympatico.ca/ray.saitz/poetry.htm) and *Virtual Seminars for Teaching Literature* (http://info.ox.ac.uk/jtap/), a British production which features a polished tutorial on the poetry of World War I.

Occasional projects that sponsor the sharing of poetry written by students are offered on the *Global Schoolhouse* Web site (http://www.gsn.org). Users should explore the search feature and the Hilites archive, which contains hundreds of collaborative projects sent in by teachers in schools throughout the world. One of the more interesting efforts I found was The Peace Poem, a United Nations-sponsored project that invited schools around the world to reflect upon the idea of peace by writing a collaborative electronic global poem. Others from the past were Found Poetry and Poetry Writing Activity. In the latter, "the high school English Department at the International School of Stavanger [Norway] invites year 9 and 10 students to participate in a poetry writing activity on the WWW. The aim of the activity is to create genuine opportunities for students to publish their writing and have other students read it."

Discussion Groups

Discussion groups (newsgroups, usenets) and listservs on poetry are also available. These are ongoing talk sessions of sorts organized around a topic of interest. Subscribers can observe (as "lurkers") or participate in "discussions" on anything concerning the topic. Probably the most popular is *rec.arts.poems,* where most participants submit original verse ("Are there any others out there who enjoy sonnets? Here are a few of mine.") for review and commentary. The talk is unfettered, uncensored, and unpredictable. Often announcements are made about meetings, readings, journals starting up, and the like ("We meet every Wednesday evening at the Three Johns Public House. . . ."). There are frequent requests:

> "I need a piece of poetry that would convey to my girlfriend that even though we are 700 miles apart, she is still in my heart."

> "I am interested in different analyses of this poem [Frost's 'Design']."

> "*Highbeams*, an online journal on the Beloit College gopher, seeks innovative poetry, fiction, and nonfiction. . . ."

> "Can anyone tell me who wrote the following lines from a poem I remember as a child?"

There are other poetry discussion groups besides rec.arts.poems. Possibly more appropriate ones for young adults, at least at this writing, are alt.teens.poetry.and.stuff and ucd.rec.poetry. Do realize, however, that discussion groups are totally democratic and free-wheeling. Don't be surprised or shocked at what shows up.

Mailing lists are similar but they require subscribing, usually by sending an e-mail to the server address. Among the poetry lists I found in a recent directory are CAP-L, a discussion of contemporary American poetry accessible by e-mailing cap-l@virginia.edu; POETRY-W, a poetry writing workshop at listserv@lists.psu.edu; and HUMOR&POETRY (requests@lists.expand.com). Young adults especially might be interested in TEEN-POETS (majordomo@cyber.citilink.com) and TEENWRITE (listserv@psuvm.psu.edu), which is a creative writing workshop for young people. Also of interest to English language arts teachers is NCTE-TALK (majordomo@serv1.ncte.org), an electronic discussion group of the National Council of Teachers of English, where issues having to do with the teaching of poetry are among the many topics of conversation.

For an updated list of newsgroups and mailing lists, access *Liszt of Newsgroups* (http://www.liszt.com/news/). Some listings include links that provide direct access.

Miscellaneous Sites

For the teacher who can't quite think of a poem but recalls a line or two, huge computerized databases are ready to help. One is the search function for *Project Bartleby Archive* cited earlier (http://www.columbia.edu/acis/bartleby/). This service will comb through the complete works of Keats, Shelley, Wordsworth, Dickinson, and Oscar Wilde plus Whitman's *Leaves of Grass*, Bartlett's *Familiar Quotations*, and other works. I typed in the word *coffee* and found eighty-four matches in thirty-four files, including Eliot's "I have measured out my life with coffee spoons" from *The Love Song of J. Alfred Prufrock*.

    Poem Finder (http://www.poemfinder.com/) is another, even larger database which catalogs over 550,000 poems, 40,000 of them in full text. Available by subscription and continually updated, *Poem Finder* locates works by title, first line, last line, book title, author, and thousands of subjects. Another search site more restricted in its focus is *The Database of African-American Poetry, 1760–1900* (http://etext.lib.virginia.edu/aapd.html), a collection of over 2,500 poems.

    Lyrics.ch: The International Lyrics Server (http://www.lyrics.ch/) is one of several homepages aimed at helping users find the lyrics to popular songs. The service has a file of almost 100,000 titles and searches authors, titles, and cassettes/CDs. When I entered "Desperado" by The Eagles, I received the song in a flash.[2]

    The Geraldine R. Dodge Poetry Festival (http://www.grdodge.org/poetry/index.html) is the Web site for the largest poetry event in North America, a biennial four-day festival of readings, discussions, and workshops in historic Waterloo Village, New Jersey. Some events are aimed at high school students and teachers.

    Glossary of Poetic Terms (http://shoga.wwa.com/~rgs/glossary.html) is exactly what it says, a dictionary of hundreds of terms defined, "pronounced," and cross-referenced.

    The Semantic Rhyming Dictionary (http://bobo.link.cs.cmu.edu/dougb). Type in a word—and presto!

    National Slam Poetry Championships (http://www.machine1.com/97nationals/) is one of the best homepages on slams. Another is *The*

International Organization of Performing Poets (http://www.slamnews.com/iopp.htm).

Dimocopo (http://student.uq.edu.au/~s271502/animgif.html) is a lively Australian Web site featuring electronic poetry, animated "poems" that dance and flicker on the screen. It's like concrete poetry come to life. This is a site to explore: take a look at "she left," "roller coaster," and "easter." But beware: one or two of these cyberpoems are R-rated.

For many critics of the Internet, this final homepage has ominous overtones. *Dimocopo* suggests a kind of far-out poetry-on-the-fringe consisting of words that gleam and vibrate on a screen. In fact for skeptics, the Internet as a whole is little more than a slick, pulsating dog-and-pony show, shallow and compelling. For others (one is reminded of the claims of many politicians), it is the beckoning answer to all our classroom problems.

Of course it is neither. For teachers of poetry, the Internet has clear limitations. It cannot write a poem, not a good one anyway. It will not teach students how to invest their work with imagination. It will not convey a love of Dickinson or Frost or Jane Kenyon. What it will do is offer information galore about poets and poetry. For poets and teachers, it will provide feedback and conversation and certain kinds of help. If it will not write poems, it will at least offer them—thousands. Here in its infancy, despite a wealth of Web sites that are worthless and beyond consideration, the Internet is a wonderful tool awaiting the imagination and resourcefulness of creative teachers who will make it even better.

Notes

1. All of the Web sites mentioned in this chapter and elsewhere in the book were accessed as recently as March 1, 1999.

2. In January 1999, the International Lyrics Server was shut down until further notice by actions taken by the National Music Publishers Association, an organization concerned with copyright infringement. Pascal De Vries, the Swiss owner of the Web site, has predicted that the conflict will be resolved in his favor. Meanwhile, teachers and others can try links to similar sites posted at <lyrics.ch>, which remains accessible sans lyrics.

II THE REEMERGENCE OF CRITICAL LITERACY

While the idea of critical literacy is rooted in the Frankfurt School's critical theory, current discussion and implementation of critical literacy can be traced to the work of the late Paulo Freire, beginning with his book *Pedagogy of the Oppressed.* Linda M. Christensen, known largely for her work with Rethinking Schools, is directly connected to Friere's ideology of critical consciousness. In her leading article, she offers a working definition of critical literacy and an exploration of the instructional paradigm she employs in her classroom. Brian Moon's entries on "Reading Practices" and "Readings" succinctly illustrate specific reading-instruction strategies through a critical lens. Griselle M. Diaz-Gemmati's "And Justice for All" highlights the importance of addressing racism as a primary focus of a critically literate classroom. In doing so, she articulates the difficult but necessary processing that must occur in a multiracial classroom. Charles Moran and Cynthia L. Selfe's discussion of the role that technology plays in the classroom enables educators to perceive the lack of neutrality in education practice and policy. They reveal the political pitfalls of uncritical use of new technological media. Finally, Randy Bomer completes this section, describing critical writing activities that engage students in observation, questioning, and reflection.

6 Critical Literacy: Teaching Reading, Writing, and Outrage

Linda M. Christensen

From history to literature to language, my teachers' choices informed me to lower my expectations. I knew that the people who changed history were great men—Columbus, Washington, Lincoln. Because no one like me or my family was included in the curriculum, I learned I wasn't important, my family wasn't important, and I shouldn't expect too much. The women who made a difference were ordained by God, like Joan of Arc, or sewed their way to fame, like Betsy Ross. I clung to those few women and claimed them as my guides. I never heard of Fannie Lou Hamer or Frida Kahlo until I started teaching.

I was from a working-class family. My mother, the eighth child out of twelve, was the first to finish high school. My father only finished grade school. I was the fourth child in my family and the first to attend college. We didn't talk right. We said "chimley" and "the-ater." We confused our verbs. In the ninth grade, Mrs. Delaney asked me to stand in front of my English class and pronounce words like "beige," or "baj," as we said. I was an example of how not to talk. I became ashamed of myself and my family.

It wasn't until I studied the history of the English language that I realized there might have been a reason, other than stupidity, laziness, or ignorance, for the way my family pronounced words and used verb tenses. And I was angry that I hadn't been taught that history, that I'd been allowed, in fact, *made*, to feel ashamed of my home language.

Today I am outraged by the experience. And I want my students to be outraged when they encounter texts, museums, commercials, classes, and

Reprinted from Chapter 10 of *Making Justice Our Project,* edited by Carole Edelsky.

rules that hide or disguise a social reality that glorifies one race, one culture, one social class, one gender, or one language, without acknowledging the historical context that gave it dominance. I want to teach a critical literacy that equips students to "read" power relationships at the same time that it imparts academic skills.

As a high school English teacher, I attempt to make my literacy work—in a predominately African American, working-class neighborhood—a sustained argument against inequality and injustice. My high school is currently scheduled to be reconstituted because of our low test scores. Of the 2,200 neighborhood students who could attend our school, only 950 do; the rest transfer to other schools districtwide. The majority of students who enter "Jeff" have not passed the eighth-grade tests in reading and writing. I write this because these numbers "say" something about my school and the state of the students who enter the building. But those scores do not tell the truth about the intelligence and ability of my students.

I use critical literacy in all three of the classes I typically teach. "Contemporary Literature and Society" and "Writing for Publication" are both untracked senior English classes that meet daily for eighty minutes, one during the fall semester and one during the spring semester. "Literature and U.S. History," an untracked eighty-minute block class I teach for the entire year, carries junior English and U.S. history credit. I typically teach the standard three-class daily load under Jefferson's block schedule, which means two sections of literature and U.S. history and one each of the senior classes. These courses carry standard English and/or history credit, so I must still follow all of the official guidelines and "standards" hoops set up outside of my classroom as I do my critical-literacy work. This term I have thirty-five students in my senior class and thirty-eight in my junior class.

Some might say that the role of language arts teachers is to teach reading, writing, and language and that we should not be worrying about issues like injustice or racism. But I would respond that the teaching of literacy is political. Any piece of literature my students pick up—from cartoons to children's books to the literature we read in class—legitimates what Chilean writer Ariel Dorfman (1983, p. 7) calls a "social blueprint" about what it means to be men, women, poor, people of color, gay, or straight. And that vision is political—whether it portrays the status quo or argues for a reorganization of society.

How and when I "correct" students' language and writing is also political. If I do not teach students that the standard language in this country, or any country, is not based on the "best" language but on the language that the powerful, the ruling class, developed, then every time I "correct" their home language I am condemning it as wrong, as incorrect, as "nonstandard." If I fail to make that social blueprint transparent, I endorse it.

No subject in school, including literature, composition, and the study of language, is "value-free," as Ira Shor points out in *A Pedagogy for Liberation* (Shor & Freire, 1987). Too often, "[t]hese falsely neutral curricula train students to observe things without judging, to see the world from the official consensus, to carry out orders without questioning, as if the given society is fixed and fine" (p. 12).

Teachers must draw students into what Brazilian educator Paulo Freire described as a "critical dialogue about a text or a moment of society . . . to reveal it, unveil it, see its reasons for being like it is, the political and historical context of the material" (Shor & Freire, 1987, p. 13). But beyond illumination, students must use the tools of critical literacy to dismantle the half-truths, inaccuracies, and lies that strangle their conceptions about themselves and others. They must use the tools of critical literacy to expose, to talk back to, to remedy any act of injustice or intolerance that they witness.

What Is Critical Literacy?

Several years ago, I attended a literature workshop at which we read a chapter from Olive Ann Burns's novel *Cold Sassy Tree* (1984). The workshop was wonderful, full of useful techniques to engage students in literature: a tea party, text rendering, writing from our own lives, using an innocent narrator as Burns does. Great methodology. And ones I use with almost every unit I teach. But the entire workshop ignored the issues of race, class, and gender that run like a sewer through the novel—from the "linthead" factory workers, to the African Americans who work as kitchen help, to the treatment of women. The workshop explored none of this.

For too many years of my teaching career, I also ignored the social text. I thought it meant talking about setting. I had not been taught anything different. Saying that the novel was set in the South during such and such a period was enough. But it is not enough. Not questioning why the lintheads and the African Americans in the novel were treated differently or not exploring the time Grandpa blamed Grandma for not bearing him a son— this allows readers to silently accept these practices as just. Young women internalize the idea that they must be beautiful and bear sons to be loved. Working-class students learn that it is their fault if they are poor like the lintheads in the novel. When I taught literature without examining the social and historical framework, I condoned the social text students absorbed.

Critical literacy does explore the social and historical framework. It moves beyond a description of society and into an interrogation of it. Why were the lintheads poor? Why weren't they accepted by the middle class? In a society that has so much, why do some starve while others get fat? Why do women have to be beautiful to be loved? Critical literacy questions the basic assumptions of our society.

In each unit of study I use the same basic format: (1) a question that provokes the examination of historical, literary, and social "texts"; (2) the study and involvement of students' lives; (3) the reading of a variety of texts, ranging from novels to historical documents, to first-person narratives, to movies, speakers, role-plays, and field trips; and (4) a final project that opens the possibility for students to act on their knowledge. Critical literacy is big and messy. It combines the reading and writing of poetry, fiction, essay, historical documents and statistics, lots of discussions, readarounds, days of writing, responding, and revising of student work.

This kind of work takes time. We cannot race through a half-dozen novels. I am forced to make difficult choices about what I include and what I leave out. Often, one novel will provide the center, or core, and I will surround it with other texts, role-plays, videos, improvisations, museum visits, or speakers.

The Question

In my "Contemporary Literature and Society" classes, we are exploring the question, "Is language political?" Why language? Because language is about power. And critical literacy is about "reading" and uncovering power relationships in the world. Whose language or dialect has power? Whose does not? Why not? What happens if someone has a Spanish or Vietnamese accent? A British accent? How does language benefit some and hurt others? Through the study of language, students look behind the Wizard of Oz machinery that ranks some languages as standard and others as substandard. We ask, whose papers get corrected for language errors and whose enter correct? How might that affect their feelings about themselves? Their language? Their family? We ask, who scores high on SATs and who doesn't? We stop pretending that grades, achievement, and high test scores are only based on a meritocracy in which everyone starts out equal. We look at how some privileges, like high SATs, might look as if they are earned, but have really been inherited on the basis of social class or race or gender. We look at pieces of literature, we read studies, and we examine our own lives as we search for answers to the question "Is language political?"

We also look at how language is embedded in culture. Language is not just about subjects and verbs; it is about music, dance, family relationships; it is about how we view the present and the future. We read Jack Weatherford's (1991) study of native languages. What might a language full of nouns tell us about a culture? How about a language full of verbs? A language with no past tense? No future tense? A language with no word for "read" or "write?" A language with two hundred words for snow? A language with six words for love?

Students' Lives at the Center

Critical literacy is embedded in students' lives just as deeply as the students' lives are embedded in this society. To teach students to read and write and think critically about "the word and the world," as Freire phrases it, means to engage them in a study of their lives in relation to the larger society. Why is it important for students to write about their lives? Why is it part of critical literacy? Why is it necessary to include student lives when studying a unit on language? Because in critical literacy, their lives are part of the text of the class. Their experience with language helps us to understand how society creates hierarchies that rank some languages as "standard" and others as "substandard"; some as "educated," others as "ignorant."

Bringing in students' language is more than a feel-good gesture; it is more than erasing the shame that comes when one's language is considered inferior. What Lois Yamanaka writes about Pidgin, I could have written about my home language and many of my students could write about their linguistic heritage—from Ebonics to Spanish to Vietnamese:

> But Pidgin, written and published Pidgin, is the evidence of the integrity of the language. What was once an indication of belonging to a particular community has become a way of validating the individuals within this community. It is impossible to ban the *sound* of one's memory. Ours is a history of coercion that alienated an entire community of Pidgin speakers. To refuse, to neglect or forfeit, the direction of the language that a voice pursues is to manipulate the person away from the self. (Yamanaka, undated)

As we discuss language and culture, the students write pieces about themselves, their homes, their family sayings, their language. We do what Yamanaka urges. We remember our homes without censoring. We read, for example, George Ella Lyon's (1996) poem "Where I'm from." We note how Lyon's poem includes details from her life—lists of items cluttering her house, a counting of the trees and bushes in her neighborhood, sayings from

her family, the names of family members, the memories of foods they ate
together. I encourage students to use their "home language" as they write.
The following excerpts are from student poems which Lyons' piece
provoked:

> I am from bobby pins, doo rags, and wide tooth combs.
> I am from prayer plants that lift their stems
> and rejoice every night.
>
> I am from chocolate cakes and deviled eggs
> from older cousins and hand-me-downs
> to "shut ups" and "sit downs"
>
> I am from Genesis to Exodus,
> Leviticus, too.
> church to church, pew to pew
>
> I am from a huge family tree that begins with dust
> and ends with me.
>
> — Oretha Storey

> I am from the little brown house
> in the city streets.
> I'm from a street
> that is much, much too tough.
>
> I am from a neighborhood
> where the crack heads roam free.
> The police never seem to harass them,
> but they always harass me.
>
> — Candace Broadnax

> I am from dust, beaches and shells,
> the coconut tree hanging over my house.
> I am from a big belly man
> and black haired woman.
> I am from an island in the Pacific.
> I am from Victoria and Scott's branch,
> breadfruit and coconut,
> the hand my grandfather cut off
> when he tried to get a coconut from the tree.
>
> — Diovina Thomas

> I am from old pictures
> and hand sewn quilts.
> I am from the Yerba Buena
> to the old walnut tree that is no more.

I am from carne con chile
to queso con tortillas.
I am from farmers and ancient Indians
to the frijoles and sopa
they ate.

— Lurdes Sandoval

I am from awapuhi ginger,
sweet fields of sugar cane,
green bananas.

I am from warm rain cascading over
taro leaf umbrellas,
crouching beneath the shield of kalo.

I am from poke, brie cheese, mango, and raspberries,
from Maruitte
and Aunty Nani.

I am from Moore and Cackley
from sardines and haupia.
From Mirana's lip Djavan split
to the shrunken belly
my grandmother could not cure.

— Djamila Moore

I am from Aztlán
where many battles and wars were fought.
I am from the strength and courage of the Aztecs
who died for our freedom.
I am from traditions and customs
from *posadas* and *quinceañeras*
to *día de la muerte* and *buena suerte*.

I am from the blood of my ancestors,
the dreams of my grandmother,
the faith of my mother,
and the pride of my culture.

I am from the survivors.

— Alejandro Vidales

I am from the land that struggles
for freedom.
I am from the rice field, water buffaloes
and cows.
I am from the place where

Blood floats like rivers
Innocent souls are trapped
under the ground
Dead bodies haven't yet been buried.
A beautiful barn becomes
a cemetery.

It wasn't supposed to be like this.

I am from the place I hold
now only a memory.
I am from a family with hearts like stones.

— Cang Dao

Why is it important to have students writing about their lives? Why is this a part of critical literacy? As Lois Yamanaka says, "With language rests culture. To sever the language from the mouth is to sever the ties to homes and relatives, family gatherings, foods prepared and eaten, relationships to friends and neighbors. Cultural identity is utterly akin to linguistic identity" (undated). Bringing students' languages, ancestors, and sayings from their homes into the classroom validates their language, their culture, and their history as topics worthy of study. It says they count; their language is part of a history that most language textbooks ignore, or worse, label as "incorrect." Speaking their languages and telling their stories breaks the pattern of silence and shame that correction without historical and linguistic context breeds. How else can we understand our society and our world if we don't bring in the lives of the people who are living it?

Reading the Word and the World

During this unit we read literature from diverse perspectives: *Wild Meat and Bully Burgers* by Lois Ann Yamanaka (1966), about the politics of Pidgin in Hawai'i; *Pygmalion* by George Bernard Shaw (1914/1951), about the politics of English in England; "How to Tame a Wild Tongue" by Gloria Anzaldúa (1987) and "Achievement of Desire" by Richard Rodriguez (1982), about the politics of English for people whose home language is Spanish. We also read segments of *Brothers and Sisters* by Bebe Moore Campbell (1994), *Talkin' and Testifyin'* by Geneva Smitherman (1997), the Ebonics issue of *Rethinking Schools* (see Perry & Delpit, 1997). We read these pieces, talk back to them, examine how the characters feel about themselves, their families, culture, and race. As they read, I ask students to take notes on their readings, to think about why one language is standard while the rest struggle under labels of "lazy," "incompetent," or "broken," to think about whose languages are in those categories and whose are not. I encourage students to "talk back" to these readings, to imagine they are in a conversation with the writer.

For example, when responding to Geneva Smitherman's article, "Black English/Ebonics: What It Be Like?" (1998), Kesha wrote, "I used to think that Ebonics meant we couldn't speak proper English, that we were dumb. I'm glad we learned the true history." Later, reading the same piece, she noted, "Reading these articles and watching the video [the video segment "Black on White" in McCrum, Cran, & MacNeil (1986)] made me realize that the words I speak and the way I speak came from my African people. I felt pride." Ebony wrote, "People don't understand Ebonies, so they call it 'ghetto' or 'slang.' They need to learn the history." Saqualla noted, "A lot of us who speak Ebonies are ashamed of our talk because the society we live in expects something different, looks down on us." Responding to the quote "Attitudes shape expectations and a teacher's expectations shape performance," Niambi wrote, "This is so true. A kid can tell if they are being treated as if they are stupid, and many times feel they must be if a teacher says they are."

Our discussions of these articles and pieces of literature spark heated debates. After reading Richard Rodriguezs "Achievement of Desire," students argue about the need to leave their culture and language behind in order to succeed. They compare Rodriguez to Esther in *Brothers and Sisters*, people who move up, "act white," and leave their culture and their people behind. Students ask: Should Lakeesia, a young mother with a desire to be a bank clerk and get off welfare, get the job even if she speaks "nonstandard English"? How much are we willing to change in order to get ahead? Is speaking Standard English acting white? Does everyone have to code switch on the job? Kesha asks, "Why we always gotta be the ones who have to change?" Goldie asks, "Why can't we be the Standard?" and Masta asks, "Who made the Standard? Who died and made them the standard makers anyway?"

I also nudge them to see if any of the characters' lives parallel the struggles they face. When students read a book that is as foreign to their lives as Shaw's Pygmalion, one of the ways they can engage in the reading is by finding similarities in their own lives, linking Eliza Doolittle's struggle with English in England and the world of my student, Jose, who crossed the border with his grandmother and a coyote when he was five years old. Even noncritical reading theory acknowledges that students must be engaged with a text in order to read it.

Later, when students write critical essays on one or more of the texts we've read during our unit on the "Politics of Language," they write about their lives as well. Alejandro and Hecmarie compare their difficulties learning English when they came to the United States and the taunts they faced with Eliza's attempts to learn "proper" English. As Alejandro writes in his literary essay:

> When I came to this country and started school, it was a new experience. When I arrived in my classroom all the kids stared at me. I had hair like the white kids, but I was darker than them. I was not black though. I was in between.
>
> I was constantly made fun of because of my accent. It seemed funny to my classmates and all the stereotypes in the cartoons would make them say stuff to me like *"Arriba! Arriba!"* This really aggravated me. Like Liza [Doolittle from *Pygmalion*]. I wanted to be respected for who I was. If it meant changing, I was willing to do it. I had to teach people who I was and make them respect me. In the process, I had to beat up a couple of kids. But even though I changed, I remembered where I came from. Liza didn't.

Denedra compares the disruptive role of alcoholism in Eliza's life with the abuse of alcohol in hers. Djamila and Jason discuss the difficulty of going "home" that both Eliza and Richard Rodriguez experience after they've become educated and their struggles to belong in two communities: Hawai'ian/mainland for Djamila and urban African American/suburban African American for Jason.

Writing the World

Creating a critical-literacy classroom still means teaching students to read and write. But instead of only asking students to write essays that demonstrate a close reading of a novel or engaging in a literary evaluation of the text, critical literacy creates spaces for students to tackle larger social issues that have urgent meaning in their lives.

As Deshawn demonstrates in the opening to his essay, these pieces can reflect the struggles students deal with daily:

> I was born black, raised black, and I live black. But now that I have achieved a job outside the general blackness, some say I'm white because of the language I choose to speak at work. Have I put my culture behind me in order to succeed?

Kaanan wrote his essay to an audience of teachers. He came alive to the study of Ebonics and its ensuing struggles in Oakland, California. He began to understand that his problems with spelling, grammar, and writing might have been influenced by home language. But he also came to see that if his teachers understood more about his "home language," they might have helped him more:

> Teachers should be able to teach students Ebonics if they want. People need to accept it. Ebonics is going to be here forever. You can't take a whole language and get rid of it. Teachers who don't know about Ebonics should learn about it so they can build better relationships with kids. Teachers would understand what kids are talking about when they speak Ebonics.
>
> When I went to school, teachers didn't really teach me how to spell or put sentences together right. They just said sound it out, so I would spell it the way I heard it at home. Everybody around me at home spoke Ebonics, so when I sounded it out, it sounded like home and it got marked wrong. When I wrote something like, "My brother he got in trouble last night," I was marked wrong. Instead of showing me how speakers of Ebonics sometimes use both a name and a pronoun but in "Standard English" only one is used, I got marked wrong. So when my teachers graded my papers, they would either put a lot of corrections on my papers or just give me a bad grade. They didn't know where I was coming from.
>
> People are going to speak and write how they hear things from home. Kids should be able to get taught both, but just know when to speak "proper" and when not to. Like when they go to a job interview, they should speak proper, but when they are at home, they should speak Ebonics. Teachers should teach kids when and where to speak Ebonics.
>
> I feel you can't take a part of someone's history and heritage away from them. In school they teach us about a lot of stuff that never happened, like when they say that Christopher Columbus discovered American. They might as well teach kids something that's real, like Ebonics, and help kids out.

Moving beyond Classroom Walls

When students are "steeped" in evidence from one of the units, they begin to write. I want them to turn their anger, their hurt, their rage into words that might affect other people. We talk about potential audiences and outlets— from parents, to teens, to corporations. Students have written pamphlets for parents to "teach" them about how to use cartoons and videos carefully with their children, articles about anorexia for middle school girls. Khalilah wrote a piece about the politics of color. Joe sent his cartoon essay off to *Essence* magazine because he wanted African American males to take note of how they are "dissed" in cartoons. Tammy wrote about the prejudice against "fat" people in our society. In our whole language classrooms, audience should not be a "pretend someone" out there. We need to find ways for our students to express their real concerns about the world.

Sometimes their writing addresses the outrage that comes when they understand that they do not need to feel the pain or shame that their "secret education" drilled into them. During the follow-up to our unit on the politics of language, students read a chapter from David Owen's book *None of the Above (1985)* called "The Cult of Mental Measurement." In this essay, Owens describes the racist past of the SATs and also points out how race continues to be a factor in these kinds of standardized tests today. Students are outraged by their discoveries. A few years ago, Frank rallied the class to go on strike and refuse to take the SATs. After a long debate, the class decided that their strike might hurt them more than it would hurt the Educational Testing Service. Several students vowed that they would not apply to any school that used the SATs as an entrance requirement.

But we did find a way to demystify the tests and use our knowledge to teach others about our outrage. I asked students to analyze each of the verbal sections of the SATs. We examined the instructions, the language, the "objectives" of each section. We looked at how the language and culture of the SATs reflected the world of upper-class society. After examining each section and taking the tests a few times, I asked students to construct their own tests using the culture, content and vocabulary of our school. A sample is reproduced in Figure 1 on page 67.[1]

After students complete the test and our unit on language, we take our tests and knowledge up to Ruth Hubbard's education classes at Lewis and Clark College. Sometimes we find other professors at local universities who welcome my students in as teachers for a day. My students "give" the preservice teachers the JAT and ask them to imagine that it is a high-stakes test that will determine their future—what college they get into, scholarships, and so on. After the tests, students discuss the issue of testing and language. In this way, my students have a real audience whose future teaching practice will hopefully be enlightened by their work. They see that what they learn in school can make a difference in the world, and so can they.

Language arts teachers need to explore more than the best practices, the newest techniques in our profession; we need to explore and question the content as well. Too often, the work of critical literacy is seen as necessary in inner-city schools or in schools where students of color represent the majority of the student body, but it is deemed unnecessary in schools where the majority of students are of European descent. I would argue that critical literacy is an emergency in these schools as well. How else are students who have only been exposed to the status quo going to recognize and resist injustice? Students must learn to identify not only how their own lives are affected by our society, but also how other people's lives are distorted or maligned by the media and by historical, literary, and linguistic inaccuracy.

Note

1. Not all of these fit exactly the prototypical SAT question. The point is to get students to understand the relationship among tests, culture, privilege, and meritocracy. This is just one vehicle for learning that lesson. Answers: (1) The "correct" answer according to Jefferson students is (d). Tony is the award given for plays. At Jefferson the Howard Cherry is awarded for excellence in sports. (2) The "correct" answer is (d). When hair gets "new growth," it needs a perm. When nails get new growth, they need a fill. (3) The "correct" answer is (a). A ranfal is a type of lowrider. Ben Davis is a type of shirt. (4) The correct answer is (c). *Red Beans and Rice* is the name of a play. Mozzarella is a kind of cheese. (5) The "correct" answer is (d). A dancebelt is worn by a male dancer to keep his "privates" in place. Boxers are loose-fitting underwear; thus, the difference between a prison and freedom. (6) The "correct" answer is (c). A hater is a person who is jealous. A gansta is a person who is ruthless.

References

Anzaldúa, G. (1987). How to tame a wild tongue. In *Borderlands/La frontera: The new mestiza* (pp. 53–64). San Francisco: Spinsters/ Aunt Lute.

Burns, O. (1984). *Cold sassy tree.* New York: Dell.

Campbell B. M. (1994). *Brothers and sisters.* New York: Putnam.

Dorfman, A. (1983). *The empire's old clothes: What the Lone Ranger, Babar, and other innocent heroes do to our minds.* New York: Pantheon.

Lyon, G. E. (1996). Where I'm from. In J. Blum, B. Holman, & M. Pellington (Comps.), *The United States of poetry* (p. 24). New York: Abrams.

McCrum, R., Cran, W., & MacNeil, R. (1986). *The story of English. Chicago*: Films Inc. 9 videocassettes (60 min. ea.).

Perry, T., & Delpit, L. (Eds.). (1997). The real Ebonics debate: Power, language, and the education of African-American children. Special issue of *Rethinking Schools*, 12(1).

Owen, D. (1985). *None of the above: Behind the myth of scholastic aptitude.* Boston: Houghton Mifflin.

Rodriguez, R. (1982). *Hunger of memory: The education of Richard Rodriguez.* Boston: Godine.

Shaw, G. B. (1914/1951). *Pygmalion: A play in five acts.* Harmondsworth, England: Penguin.

Shot, L, & Freire, P. (1987). *A pedagogy for liberation: Dialogues on transforming education.* South Hadley, MA: Bergin & Garvey.

Smitherman, G. (1997). *Talkin' and testifyin': The language of black America.* Rpt. ed. Boston: Houghton Mifflin.

Yamanaka, L. (undated). The politics of Pidgin. Promotional material. New York: Farrar, Straus & Giroux.

Yamanaka, L. (1996). *Wild meat and bully burgers.* New York: Farrar, Straus & Giroux.

Weatherford, J. (1991). "Americanization of the English language." In *Native Roots: How the Indians Enriched America* (pp. 195–213). New York: Crown Publishers.

Recommended Sources

Baca, J. S. (1995). So Mexicans are taking jobs from Americans. In J. Daniels (Ed.), *Letters to America: Contemporary American poetry on race (p. 29).* Detroit: Wayne State University Press.

Crawford, J. (1992). *Hold your tongue: Bilingualism and the politics of English only.* Reading, MA: Addison-Wesley.

Dunbar, P L. (1994). *We wear the mask. In Search of Color Everywhere* (p. 72). New York: Stewart, Tabori, & Chang.

Espada, M. (Ed.). (1994). *Poetry like bread: Poets of the political imagination from Curbstone Press.* Willimantic, CT: Curbstone Press.

Jordan, J. (1988). Nobody mean more to me than you and the future life of Willie Jordan. *Harvard Educational Review,* 58(3), pp. 363–374.

McDaniel, W E. (1994). *Who said we all have to talk alike?* In L. King (Ed.), *Hear my voice: A multicultural anthology of literature from the United States* (p. 7). Menlo Park, CA: Addison-Wesley.

Walker, A. (1982). *The color purple.* New York: Washington Square.

JAT

Jefferson Achievement Test

Each question below consists of a related pair of words or phrases, followed by four lettered pairs of words or phrases. Select the lettered pair that best expresses a relationship similar to that expressed in the original pair.

---

1. Tony : Play ::
   (a) Broadway : Annie
   (b) Oscar : Tom Hanks
   (c) Brandon : Soccer
   (d) Howard Cherry : sports

2. New Growth : Perm ::
   (a) press : straight
   (b) weave : long
   (c) corn row : braid
   (d) nails : fill

3. Ranfal : Lowrider ::
   (a) Ben Davis : shirt
   (b) Mexico : cold
   (c) Mexican : brown
   (d) Cuete : gun

4. *Red Beans and Rice* : Play ::
   (a) corn and tortillas : run
   (b) song : dance
   (c) mozzarella : cheese
   (d) sonata : musical

5. Dancebelt : Boxers ::
   (a) shoes : socks
   (b) student : teacher
   (c) leotard : leg warmers
   (d) prison : freedom

6. Hater : Jealous ::
   (a) love : fighter
   (b) peacemaker : unrest
   (c) gangsta : ruthless
   (d) fighter : chaos

Figure 1. JAT Student-Constructed Test.

7 Reading Practices/Readings

Brian Moon

Reading Practices

To Get You Thinking

- Each of these four puzzles represents a common word, phrase, or popular saying. Can you work them out?

A	B	C	D
R E A D I N G	Z E Z E B R A R A	V I S I O N	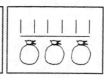

- When you have the answer, try stating some "rules" that will tell people how to read this kind of puzzle.

Rules:

1. _____

2. _____

3. _____

Theory

Reading a literary text can be likened to the process of solving the puzzles printed above. Readers process the visual information provided to them by applying a set of rules. In the example above, some of the rules might be:

- the placing of letters and words often represents a preposition (for example; below, above, between);

- single letters often refer to words with the same sound (for example; I = eye); and so on.

The rules which readers apply to a text are not personal and unique. They are normally shared by members of a community. The application of a shared set of rules is known as a *reading practice*, and reading practices are the strategies by which readers make sense of a text. Because most of us learn these rules at an early age, and because we apply them to so many texts, we tend to forget that we are using a set of rules at all. Instead, reading comes to seem "natural." The process of reading is, however, quite complicated. In reading a literary text, readers commonly do all of the following:

- decode words and phrases according to dominant meanings;

- look for patterns of repetition and description, and interpret these as meaningful symbols or images;

- invent connections between words and phrases so as to build up a "complete" world from the limited details in the text;

- construct an imaginary speaker for the writing (the narrator);

- treat the characters as imaginary people whose thoughts and actions can be judged;

- pay attention to some features of the text and ignore others, using past reading experiences as a guide; and so on.

Because texts provide a very limited amount of material to work with, readers supplement the text with background information provided by the beliefs, values, and practices of their culture. In many cases, readers do this so well, and agree with one another so closely about their readings of a text, that the whole process seems perfectly natural and obvious. When this happens, we say that the readers are using a dominant or naturalized reading practice—one which "plays by the same rules" as the text.

However, some people may choose to work with a *resistant reading practice*—that is, a way of reading which changes the rules and works "against the grain" of the text. Resistant reading is a refusal to play by the conventional rules. Like an audience that heckles a bad magician by exposing his tricks, resistant readers challenge the text by taking a sceptical approach. Resistant reading means refusing to accept the illusion that the text has an obvious meaning, or that it is complete and whole. Instead, it focuses on the gaps, silences, and contradictions which are present in all texts. The aim of resistance is usually to highlight beliefs and values which would be taken for granted in a dominant reading.

Practice

Here is an extract from *Heart of Darkness* by Joseph Conrad. It is part of the story narrated by Marlow, a sailor, who tells of his adventures in Africa.

> Now when I was a little chap I had a passion for maps. I would look for hours at South America, or Africa, or Australia, and lose myself in all the glories of exploration. At that time there were many blank spaces on the earth, and when I saw one that looked particularly inviting on a map (but they all look that) I would put my finger on it and say, When I grow up I will go there. The North Pole was one of these places, I remember. Well I haven't been there yet, and shall not try now. The glamour's off. But there was one yet—the biggest, the most blank, so to speak—that I had a hankering after.

Following are two very different readings of the extract, produced by two critics.

1. Conrad has given us an image from his own childhood—the blank map, waiting to be filled in—as a window onto Marlow's character, and a figure which draws us to him through the human spirit of adventure. For Marlow is the adventurer in all of us, and it is the timeless lure of the unexplored that makes a sea story so fascinating. Charlie Marlow, while unique and individual, represents the brave men of all ages—Columbus, Marco Polo, James T. Kirk—whose exploits touch something deep within us all.

2. *Heart of Darkness* reproduces the values of European imperialism. Those "blank spaces" were never blank; they were filled with people who the European powers simply chose to ignore. This "blankness" is the myth which all colonial powers promote to excuse their invasions. The book also reproduces masculine fantasies of domination. The "civilizing" of "primitive" cultures, like the "taming" of wives is all about imposing one's will to dominate others. It is no accident that "unexplored" continents are so often portrayed as mysterious "feminine" realms.

Each of these readings has been produced through a certain reading practice—a set of rules for making sense of the text.

1. Sort the following rules into two groups: those used by critic 1, and those used by critic 2.

    • Read the text as the expression of the author's own ideas and experiences.   _____

    • Read the text as a comment about human nature.   _____

    • Read the text as evidence of struggles between different groups of people.   _____

    • Treat characters in the text as human beings, and identify with their experiences.   _____

    • Read the text's images as developing a theme or idea.   _____

    • Challenge the validity and acceptability of images in the text. _____

    • Read the text as a patchwork of dominant cultural beliefs and values.   _____

    • Treat characters merely as devices used to develop ideas in the text.   _____

2. Which of the critics seems to offer a dominant reading? Which offers a resistant reading?

Summary

Reading practices are the processes and cultural assumptions which readers use in making sense of a text. Different practices applied to the same text will produce different readings. The choice of one practice over another depends upon the reader's training, which is determined by social factors such as education, cultural background, and dominant *ideologies*.

Readings

To Get You Thinking

    • Three people watching a football game have been asked to explain what this cultural activity means. They are a sociologist, a psychologist, and an art critic. What is each person's answer?

1. Football is a competition in which players strive to achieve certain goals within a set of limits established by the rules. It is a ritual which reminds the audience of social values such as individual effort and the importance of success.
   Who?

2. Football is a kind of dramatic narrative which aims to entertain the audience. It has heroes and villains, a story, and lots of action. Sport of this kind is a modern form of theater.
   Who?

3. Football is an acting-out of certain male anxieties. It is a socially acceptable way for grown men to play together and keep company without having their masculinity questioned. It also provides an outlet for repressed homosexual impulses.
   Who?

Theory

Any cultural "text"—from football to poetry to marriage ceremonies—can mean different things to different groups of people. This is not because we all have personal or individual opinions, but because different groups might read the text in different ways. These different ways or *practices* of reading produce ways of thinking about a text which we can call *readings*. In the activity above you have seen three different readings of a football game.

Readings are meanings which are constructed *for* a text; they are not extracted from it. The readings we construct for a text relate to the ways of thinking and acting that are made available to us by our culture, our social positions, our genders, our professions, and so on. Readers often assume that the meanings they make are merely "common sense." But what we call common sense is itself made up of readings about aspects of the world—readings which provide us with "ready-made" ways of thinking.

For any specific text, some readings will be common, others will be rare. We can suggest three classes of reading.

- Dominant or preferred readings—these are readings which the text is designed to favor, and which represent the beliefs and values which are most powerful in a culture.

- Alternative readings—these are readings which are less common but acceptable, because they do not challenge the dominant reading.

- Oppositional or resistant readings—these are readings which are unable in terms of the dominant cultural beliefs, and which challenge prevailing views.

Dominant readings are vigorously promoted through institutions such as the media, the law, education, and business, and are given privileged status. Alternative and oppositional readings tend to be marginalized, which means they circulate among smaller or less powerful groups of people.

Practice

Printed below is a summary of a "romantic" fairy tale. Before you read it, however, think about the *dominant readings* of romance in your culture.

1. Circle the dominant "romantic" reading for each of the following.

True love:	is never fulfilled	
	wins out in the end	
	doesn't really exist	
Princes:	wealthy	shallow
	charming	well educated
	beautiful	boring
Princesses:	wealthy	beautiful
	tragic	well dressed
	intelligent	snobbish
Male desire:	a desire for beautiful women	
	a desire for intelligent women	
	a desire for children	
Female desire:	a desire to be loved	
	a desire to be married	
	a desire to be independent	

Now read the summary of "Cinderella" which follows.

Cinderella lives with three stepsisters who are jealous of her beauty and who will not let her out of the house. One day, news arrives that the prince is holding a fabulous ball. The three stepsisters all go to the ball, each hoping that the prince will fall in love with her. Cinderella is left at home, but her fairy godmother appears and magically provides her with beautiful clothes and a carriage so that she can go to the ball. The spell will last only until midnight. **Cinderella**

is the most beautiful woman at the ball, and the prince will dance only with her. She rushes out of the ballroom on the stroke of twelve, however, leaving only a glass slipper behind. The prince keeps the slipper and searches the land looking for its owner. When he comes to the home of the three stepsisters, each tries to force her foot into the slipper, but fails. The prince does not recognise Cinderella in her rags, but she is permitted to try the shoe also. When it fits, she is again transformed. The prince pleads with Cinderella to marry him, and she does.

2. The story contains numerous "gaps." For example, the sentence which is in bolder type gives us two facts but does not state the link between them. Readers must fill this gap by supplying the appropriate romantic reading. Which of the readings below fills the gap? (Refer to your answers to activity number 1 if necessary.)

- true love
- prince
- male desire
- female desire

To construct a dominant (that is, romantic) reading for the story, readers supply dominant readings from their culture to fill gaps in the text.

3. Here are two readings of "Cinderella."

a. The story presents an ideal image of romantic love. It shows that true love will prevail no matter what the odds, and it encourages people to believe that dreams can come true. The story encourages an optimistic outlook on life.

b. The story is about the shallowness of men who judge women solely on the basis of physical attractiveness. A man who will marry a woman on the basis of a few hours dancing is likely to leave her just as quickly. No wonder most of the women in the story are bitter. This should be read as a cautionary tale against the idea of romantic love.

The first of these is a dominant reading; the second is a resistant or oppositional reading. Go back to activity number 1 and underline the readings which have been used in constructing the oppositional reading of the text. Does the oppositional reading also make use of "available" ways of thinking?

4. What happens if we rewrite the "Cinderella" story, filling in the gaps with the required readings of men, women, and romance? For example:

> Cinderella was the most beautiful woman at the ball. The prince loved beautiful women and always wanted to be near them, so when he saw her he would dance with no one else.

How does this rewriting change the preferred reading of the prince?

5. Go back to the three readings of football at the beginning of this entry. Can you say which is the dominant, alternative, and oppositional reading of football?

Summary

Readings are the meanings produced when a reader applies a particular reading practice to make sense of a text or some other element in the culture. Readings can also be established "ways of thinking" about some aspect of the world.

8 "And Justice for All": Using Writing and Literature to Confront Racism

Griselle M. Diaz-Gemmati

I was beginning my 10th year as an educator. I smile as I remember entering this school for the first time; my very first teaching assignment. I recall my apprehension. A Latina teacher in an Anglo neighborhood, hired to teach a handful of bused kids in a Spanish bilingual program that spanned grades one through eight. The school's community is in a White neighborhood at the edge of the Chicago city limits. It is a place that borders and looks like the suburbs, but is within the city limits and gives the city's police and firefighters the job's required city address. I was insecure and inexperienced, but determined.

I overlooked the often inadequate and sometimes nonexistent materials, the makeshift classroom, and the school clerk's bigoted rudeness. Resourcefulness soon replaced my fears. My bilingual program became a working reality of a multiage, student-directed curriculum.

I dreaded the moment when my kids left my classroom and entered the mainstream student population; it was then that I saw a rekindled look of apprehension and fear in their eyes. I taught them how to stand, but I could not follow through to watch them run.

Three years after I first walked into the school, I told the principal that I would be interested in the newly vacated eighth-grade teaching position, and he agreed to place me in a regular classroom. But the old feelings of uneasiness assaulted me once more. What would the community think? What would they say about a Latina teacher taking over the eighth-grade

Originally published as Chapter 3 of *Inside City Schools*, edited by Sarah Warshauer Freedman et al., a co-publication of NCTE and Teachers College Press. Copyright 1999 Teachers College, Columbia University.

class? Surprisingly, it was not the community that had misgivings about my ability, but my own faculty, the people I considered my colleagues. They were a group of very traditional Anglo teachers who had about 100 years of teaching experience among them. Some were bold enough to ask me outright if I was qualified to teach typical subjects in a "regular" classroom.

My apprehension developed into a passion for success. Their trepidation became my motivation. That was 6 years, twelve teachers, and three principals ago. Again I had withstood challenge and did not fail.

I was awakened from my ruminations by my eighth graders sauntering into the classroom. Although it was the 2nd day of the new school year, I knew each of them well. I had been their seventh-grade teacher the previous year. My new principal and I were concerned about this group. They had been subjected to a parade of teachers during their fifth and sixth grades. They were not cooperative; they lacked motivation, and they took no initiative. We decided that I should follow them for 2 years to see what impact, if any, I could have on them academically and emotionally. The risk paid off. This class was becoming a cohesive group of adolescents who were well liked by the entire faculty. I had grown attached to them and was glad that my opportunity to embark on a research project included this particular group.

I began my research by asking a specific, and I thought noncontroversial, question: What happens when adolescent students begin to explore the themes of racism and prejudice as they discuss and write about literature? Specifically, can they separate how they feel from what they have heard from their family, friends, and communities?

Before I relate our story, I would like to share some information about my kids. My class consisted of 33 students—19 girls and 14 boys. Of this total, 21 were bused from inner-city schools. The class's median age was 13.8. The ethnic demographics of my group were 15 African Americans (of these, one had a Latino parent and another had a European American parent), 10 European Americans, 6 Latinos, 1 Asian-American (who had one European American parent), and 1 student of East Indian heritage. I used a combination of school records and student's self labels to identify them ethnically. The class's reading abilities, according to standardized test scores, ranged from the latter part of 4th grade to the beginning of 11th grade.

My class was part of a unique school of 260 students, with one grade per class and one class per grade. The school is a microcosm of the idealistically integrated community of the future. Our realm encompasses students in a beautiful blend of colors and cultures, including a small number of special education and physically challenged students.

We are an urban school set in an open nine-acre campus on the northwest edge of the city. All of our students love the sprawling grass playgrounds where softball, soccer, football, and basketball games are played simultaneously. For our bused children, who make up about 48% of the school population, the setting contrasts sharply with the black-topped, gang-ridden, fenced-in playgrounds of many schools in their neighborhoods. I enjoy the opportunity to watch the students play with their schoolmates on self-chosen teams during the daily 15-minute morning recess or 45-minute lunch break.

Of three neighborhood public schools in this northwest area of the city, ours is the only one that is truly, and according to federal law, desegregated. The immediate neighborhood at first did not look at our integration with favor. Yet our nine acres were our sheltered zone, our paradise. It seemed to work. The kids were getting along. Their fights seemed to be the minor rumblings of dubiously scored points, ignored rules, or rowdy games of "Johnny Tackle" rather than directed racial instances.

As the eighth-grade teacher, I relish the task of putting the finishing touches on all who graduate from our school. I try to assure my students that their final year of elementary school will be not only enlightening and challenging, but memorable. It's a teacher's utopia. I consider it an advantage to be able to work with these ethnically diverse children from varying socioeconomic levels, with different children brought together in one place to work, study, play, and coexist during their grammar school years.

I embarked on my journey of teacher research with a single focus. I wanted to showcase my kids—a group of 33 fabulous adolescents who had responded enthusiastically to a literature-based, student-directed curriculum. Before me, I had all the ingredients of a thousand success stories. I initiated my research certain that it was going to be effortless. I actually believed that all I would need to do was state what I thought was the obvious. I held fast to the belief that all children can overlook their physical, ethnic, and cultural differences, if all the conditions for learning are just so. I truly believed that if they were provided with a nonpartisan, caring, and safe environment anything was possible. As I look back to the beginning of my study, I wonder, was this my reality, or was it all an illusion?

The rude awakening that my students and I experienced as a result of my research caused havoc in our classroom, on our playground, in our homes, in our communities. I find it difficult and agonizing to talk about our transition. Truthfully, the mere thought of committing the story to paper leaves me raw and emotionally depleted. I could not begin to narrate our experience without first admitting to feeling like an imbecile. How could I not have detected the snags in this magical, imaginary fabric I had woven? What was I thinking? Seeing? Ignoring?

I'll begin by providing some information about how my classes work. First, to establish a student-directed reading environment, I organize an individualized literature program. All students are responsible for selecting their own novels. They keep a log of what they have read and a journal in which they react to and critique what they are reading. They also are responsible for reporting their reading progress to the members of their literature group. Because our school offers its teachers extended class periods, I can provide a daily 20- to 25-minute sustained silent reading time. We have a reading rug where students can sit or lie down on throw pillows they have brought from home, as they read silently. I want them to get comfortable and relaxed when they read. I believe that this atmosphere fosters a pleasant and inviting attitude toward what the students once believed was a tedious task.

Literature discussions usually take place two to three times a week. The literature groups consist of five to seven members of varying reading abilities. I make sure that the members of each literature circle contain both boys and girls, from different ethnic groups, with varied reading skills and interests. Sometimes I choose their groups, and sometimes I help them with their choice. Each circle is responsible for selecting a scribe and a leader. The scribe records in the group's journal what each of the members is reading and the group members' reactions to each piece of literature. The leader prompts each member to talk about different literary aspects of the book, such as character analysis, setting, plot, and the like.

The literature leader keeps everyone's comments to a specific time limit, usually no more than 3 to 5 minutes, and briefs the entire class on the discussions that have taken place during his or her meeting. Responsibilities shift every 2 weeks or so to assure that everyone gets an opportunity to be a leader and a scribe. Since five literature circles meet at once, I go from one to the next as an observer and as a member, not as a supervisor. I really get a charge from listening to my students discuss literature from different perspectives and watching them attempt to substantiate their opinions with passages from their novels. When I am part of the group, I share my reactions to whatever novel I happen to be reading and relate my reactions to the author's writing. My students feel empowered by the ability to choose what they read.

Once the independent reading workshop becomes part of our daily routine, I initiate class novels into the program. The routine for reading a class novel is the same as for independent reading, except that now everyone reads the same novel. Reading the same piece of literature helps the class build an intellectual community as we share common reading experiences. We get to know and discuss characters we all are familiar with. Together we interpret the same dialogues and discuss the structure of a commonly known plot. I still assign independent reading for homework. The record keeping for both readings remains entirely the responsibility of the individual student.

To assist the students with the choice of a class novel, I present them with a list of prospective paperbacks on the same general theme as well as a brief synopsis of each of the suggested titles. The students then select the novel by a majority vote. Usually they elect to read something I recommend, but there are times when they negotiate with me to select a book they've heard about that isn't on my list.

To understand what happens when my adolescent students explore themes of racism and prejudice as they discuss and write about literature, I wanted my class to read two novels, *To Kill a Mockingbird* (Lee, 1960) and *Roll of Thunder, Hear My Cry* (Taylor, 1978), both of which deal with racial prejudice, but from different perspectives. I had read *To Kill a Mockingbird* years before and was haunted for weeks by its poignancy. Scout, the main character and narrator, is a prepubescent girl who is not afraid to speak her mind. Her relationship with her father is unique, and at several junctures in the novel, she flagrantly opposes her father's opinions. Scout is one of two children in a one-parent family, something I felt many of my students could relate to. I was also intrigued by the subtle understanding that the nucleus and mother figure in this White family was their Black maid, Calpurnia. I planned to use class discussions, student journals, audio recordings of literature circle discussions, student writing assignments, and written reflections of what I observed in class as the data for my research.

I first initiated a strong campaign to kindle interest in *To Kill a Mockingbird*. I lobbied for my choice by announcing to the class, "There's this novel I've read about a man who gets accused of rape. At his trial, all evidence points to his innocence. It becomes increasingly obvious to the reader that this accused man is physically incapable of committing this horrendous act of violence."

"What happens to him?" asked Nick.

"Well," I answered, "I'd rather you read the book to find out."

The class emitted a mixture of moans and chuckles.

"Mrs. Gemmati!" smiled Melissa, "Why do you do us like that? OK, I'm curious, where's this book?"

After 2 years with the same class, I felt that I had a good understanding of their group dynamics. Still, I did not want the students to feel as if they were forced into reading the novel, so I had an alternate plan. Had I felt strong resistance, I planned to organize a group of interested students to read the novel and derive my research data from their responses and reactions. I knew that the ideal situation was to have the entire class participate, but I would not have compromised my integrity or risked the students' trust. Fortunately, though, the whole group was eager to begin with *To Kill a Mockingbird*. After the paperbacks were distributed, I let the kids skim through them for a while, encouraging them to read the back cover. Some asked me questions about the time in history when this story takes place. We talked informally about the South, especially after the Civil War. We discussed mockingbirds. We reviewed and shared our general knowledge about Alabama.

I deliberately focused at first on injustice rather than on racial prejudice. I wanted my students to arrive, if they ever did, at the topic of racism by themselves.

After their initial reading assignments, the students' enthusiasm to read *To Kill a Mockingbird* varied. Some were hesitant to start such a "fat" book; others waded through its heavy metaphoric descriptions as if trying to sprint through water, but ultimately, the animated discussions that started coming from the literature circles were well worth these early difficulties.

Initially, everyone was on equal footing. Everyone seemed to pick apart the literal meaning of the words and phrases in the reading assignments. During class discussions, we explained the descriptions of Maycomb to each other. Some of the metaphors Lee uses were taken quite literally by some students. When we discussed the description "tired old town," I was amused to discover that some children envisioned a town of elderly people.

Then something altered the discussions. I happened to be sitting in on a circle discussion when a major disagreement erupted between two of my top students. The word *nigger* offended the White students in the circle much more than the Black students. Shelly, who is White, brought up this point in the discussion. In not so many words, she let her circle know that it was one of those words everyone knew, but did not use. Nancy, who is Black, resented Shelly's taking offense.

"I don't see what your problem is," she sarcastically responded to Shelly. "No one ever called you guys nothing but 'Master.'"

Shelly insisted, "Doesn't it bother you to see that vulgarity in print?"

"No, why should it?" retorted Nancy. "We know where we come from."

At this point I asked Nancy if she or people she knew addressed each other by the term *nigger* and how she felt about it.

"It don't bother us. We know we mean no harm by it."

"Then why does it tick you off when I get offended by it?" Shelly persisted.

"It takes on a different meaning coming from you," Nancy snapped.

I was perplexed. I felt that it was one of those things that many people wondered about, yet never vocalized for fear of being misinterpreted. Shelly did not possess the inhibition I felt. I asked Nancy to explain what she meant by her remark, "It takes on a different meaning coming from you."

She thought for a moment before she replied, "Mrs. Gemmati, it's like different. If my mama is complaining about her boyfriend and calls him an ass, that's OK. But if I call him an ass, she gets all over me. It's like that."

Still, Shelly refused to give ground. "It's like using a swear word."

"It depends who's doing the swearing!" Nancy shot back.

The battle lines were drawn. Others joined the fray. Soon the group was talking at rather than to each other. The rest of the discussion volleyed back and forth around the conjecture that the word *nigger* was a White man's way of ensuring the imposed lower status of the Black man. It also touched upon how some Blacks refer to each other as *nigger* without offense because they share common ground. I sat back dumbfounded. Being neither Black nor White, I felt inept at defusing the mounting tension. Yet I knew exactly what Nancy was talking about. I too used nuances with relatives and close friends that would take on an abrasive tone if used by someone other than a Puerto Rican.

The bell reverberated in the hallway, but no one paid attention. The discussion was becoming a heated argument. I felt that I had to intervene. I knew the issue was unresolved, but there was no getting them past this one point without appearing to side with one person or the other. I uneasily shooed them out to recess. A heavy tension lingered in the room for the rest of the morning. The final entry in my journal that day was, "God, what have I gotten us into?"

My drive home felt unusually long that evening. The discussion from Nancy and Shelly's literature circle was on constant replay in my mind. I couldn't drown it out. My resolve to do something about it was overwhelming. A strong part of my personality consists of being nonconfrontational. This was uncomfortable territory, and I didn't enjoy finding myself in this predicament. I wanted to discuss my situation with someone and thought of contacting some of my teacher friends but was apprehensive about their reactions. After quite a bit of deliberation, I decided to keep this incident to myself.

I arrived at school early the next morning. The previous night's fitful sleep did nothing to enhance my usual grouchy morning disposition. I listened to my voice making the morning announcements. It sounded terse. The students seemed edgy. Was I imagining this tension, or was it really still there?

The morning's opening activities went on as usual. Larry collected the lunch orders, Maria passed out journals, Jose took attendance, Freddy watered the plants, Shelly vacuumed the reading rug. The rest of the students talked among themselves as is their custom. When the chores were done, we quieted down to start writing in our personal journals. Twice I attempted to write. Nothing came. The stark white page dared me to write about my inner turmoil. I couldn't. I said a silent prayer and stood up to start the class.

"Today I'd like you to help me do a word cluster." The exercise was not new to the class. I often use this procedure to introduce new vocabulary. I find it can help the kids understand words or phrases in context and individually. The students' stirrings told me that they were fishing in their desks for their thesauruses and dictionaries. "Put them away," I announced over my shoulder as I turned toward the blackboard. "You'll only need your honest opinions and beliefs for this cluster." I printed the word "stereotype" on the board. The class sat strangely still for a few moments. The members of Nancy and Shelly's literature group silently stared at the word. Other hands around them shot up.

"A belief about something."

"A notion."

"A judgment."

The chalk in my hand tap-danced as I hurriedly wrote their responses on the blackboard.

"Is a stereotype good or bad?" I prompted.

"Bad!" was their chorused reply

"Why?" I attempted to look directly at each of them in turn as I spoke.

"Because," Nancy spoke for the first time that morning, "it's like saying all blondes are dumb." Shelly's head flew up and her icy blue glare bore into Nancy's face.

Fearing a repeat of yesterday's heated discussion, I quickly wrote the word *prejudice* next to our first cluster.

"OK, now let's cluster this word." Did my voice sound as tense as I felt?

"White."

"Black."

"Hispanic."

"Hindu."

"Chinese."

Again I hurriedly wrote on the board. After a moment, I stood still, with my back toward the class. I ignored the names of the other ethnic groups that were shouted out. Ultimately, the room settled into an uneasy silence.

"What," I asked, still facing the blackboard, "do any of these ethnic groups have to do with the meaning of the word *prejudice*?" I slowly turned to face a group of kids I thought I knew.

"Blacks hate Whites."

"Whites hate everyone," someone abruptly countered.

"The word in question is not hate!" I snapped harshly. Again I tried to look directly into each of their faces. The strained tone of my voice did not elicit any other comments or responses. I felt they had plenty to say, yet I knew that the general tone of their answers was not conducive to a productive discussion.

Thinking I might be able to diffuse some of the tension by stopping the whole class discussion, I said automatically, "Get in your literature circles, and cluster the word *prejudice* with your groups." Divide and conquer. Was that what I wanted to do?

As was my usual practice for my teacher research when students worked in groups, I went around to each group to set up tape recorders. The last thing I wanted to do was interfere or disrupt their discussions. I did not want my presence to infuse their answers with whatever responses they'd think I would want. As I later listened to the tapes of their circle discussions, I felt like an intruder. I felt as if I were eavesdropping on something confidential, something personal.

Their discussions that morning bounced back and forth for nearly half an hour. I asked each group to instruct its scribe on precisely what the members wanted to report to the whole class. I hoped that this impromptu system of channeled reporting would harness some of the negative energy that threatened to ignite my classroom.

Issues on the prejudice of gender, age, religion, race, and roles surfaced in these class reports. In a fervent circle discussion, Allen, a Black student, helped everyone realize a very important truth.

"Today's society," he reasoned, "makes us be prejudiced against each other." He stood up to emphasize his point when the others in the circle told him he was way off base.

"If you see a big guy," he directed his comments to the girls in his circle, "with a black, bulky leather jacket, face not shaved, funny looking eyes, earrings on, hands in his pockets, walking over in you direction when you on a street, and it's getting dark and you alone, don't tell me you ain't going to be scared. You going to imagine the worse, and you going to try to get out of his way. Right?"

The group did not respond.

"Hell," he continued, "even the cops say we should report stuff like that . . . call if we see anybody suspicious. Who gets to define suspicious? Our prejudices!"

Not one person countered Allen's argument. They felt he had a valid point.

For a while the scribes, holding true to our literature circle procedure, kept personal attacks at bay. Although the intensity of the students' convictions ebbed slightly during our attempts at proper classroom etiquette, it flowed just as profusely beneath the surface of our decaying facade.

In *To Kill a Mockingbird*, the attitude of White townspeople toward Blacks and those who helped Blacks sparked heated exchanges in literature circles. I tried to put everything in a historic perspective by having my students research the Jim Crow practices. I also attempted to explain the social, economic, and moral climate of the South after Reconstruction. I by no means tried to assuage the feelings of frustration the class felt when they realized the way the Blacks were regarded and treated. The students could not comprehend the flagrant disregard for human dignity the White townspeople displayed toward the Blacks.

Alas, common ground! Everyone agreed that the treatment of Blacks in the South during that period of history was deplorable. The students of color felt angry and vengeful. Their journals and writings reflected one common underlying theme—pent-up resentment. The White students felt defensive and their writings told me that they were angered and confused about their feelings.

I convinced myself that if I prompted my students to channel their energies into their reading logs and journals, I could help them deal with their anger. My strategy helped, and I watched their writings take on a new, sharper hue. They exposed themselves to me in a way that was personal, sad, and confidential. They shared dismal chunks of their lives through the silent monologue of their pens. They pressed their secrets between the sacred pages of their personal writings.

Mary, an African American girl, confessed to being afraid of fights, arguments, and confrontations. She related that her literature circle forced her to take stands on issues through combinations of unrelenting stares and uncomfortable silences. Her opinions were carefully neutral; she was afraid of being wrong. Her pent-up rage exploded several times during circle discussions, and she completely lost control. Her question to me in one journal entry will plague me forever: "Why you have to bring all this garbage into the classroom? This was the only place I could be without being made to think about stuff like who don't like who. Why you doing this to us?"

Her question pelted me with regrets. "Why was I doing this to one of the best classes I had ever had? What was I doing to them? What was I doing to me?" I wanted to cancel my commitment to the research at this juncture. After long periods of reflection, I knew I couldn't. I had pushed too far. We had heard too much. The students and I would never—could never—go back to the place we were before the project started. We needed to finish what I had started to obtain some sort of closure. It would have been cruel of me to evoke these feelings in my students and then abruptly try to reestablish the relationships we had before the research began. I continued the research, but was anxious about it.

The accusation of rape in the novel was another burning issue during circle discussions. Once again my class divided itself into separate camps— this time the dividing factor was gender.

The issue was not whether the character Luella was raped. Obviously she wasn't. The problem was the attitude of several males in the classroom:

"If she wanted Robinson that bad, he should have done it. After all, he was convicted of the crime anyway."

This viewpoint made me seethe. The girls were angrier still. It was difficult to keep my emotions from interfering in their discussions. Many times I abruptly left a circle whenever a comment I passionately disagreed with was made. The girls brought up the issue of prejudice again.

"If a girl talks or dresses a certain way, it's your belief that she's asking to be raped if she doesn't agree to a man's advances?" Nancy was livid.

A student with a police officer in his family brought in a graphic description of a rape from an actual police report. Slowly and carefully, I tried to steer these boys clear of the ignorant, but generally accepted, assumption that rape is a crime of passion. I quietly reminded the class of the number of innocent children, including boys of all ages, who are violated or molested every year. Some male students defended their belief that the punishment for rape depended on who the victim was.

Discussions continued to volley back and forth. Shelly sarcastically reminded the boys that all female victims were someone's mother, sister, daughter. "Pray it never happens to anyone you love." Her words were tainted with acid. Some boys started mumbling among themselves.

Nancy commented that Black men in the old days were done away with for looking at a White woman, and those stupid ones who went with White women were "killed like dogs in the street." But any White man could do what he wanted to a Black woman.

I don't know what prompted Larry to say, "Joe's mother's White."

Before I knew it Larry and Joe were exchanging blows in the middle of the classroom. I watched frozen with shock as they rolled over each other on the floor. Once I could get to where the melee was taking place, I found myself incapable of separating them. Nancy appeared, as if from nowhere, and grabbed one boy from behind. They got to their feet and continued exchanging blows. Nancy somehow got one of the boys into a full Nelson while I pressed the other to the wall with all my strength.

"Go ahead," she yelled, "Kill each other off. Isn't that what we doing to ourselves? Isn't that why we have no Black brothers hanging around? How many of you got your daddy home? Black men can't discuss nothing without killing each other. No wonder we in such a sorry state."

A hush fell over the classroom. I was shocked. No one except Nancy had tried to stop the fight. I was so disappointed. Holding back tears, I barked commands at the students. Everyone was to sit absolutely still at their own seats until the bell rang. In a choked voice I told the students to ask themselves why they did nothing to help Nancy and me intervene. During the final 15 minutes of that day not one student met my furious gaze.

In the quiet aftermath of a classroom left in utter disarray, long after I heard the buses pull away from the curb, I wrote in my journal: "The violence of today's society has permeated our classroom."

The novel was finished, much to my relief. I sat and pondered the ramifications of our discussions on our class. I knew that the kids' feelings were still raw. Yet they seemed hesitant to let the issue go. I asked the class if there was some unresolved sentiment about the novel that we had not explored. One question that stirred up an animated discussion was "Were the children in the novel prejudiced?"

All in the class agreed that they were not. The students observed that the kids in the book saw the town recluse more as a mystery than anyone to be shunned. They also realized that the children believed in Robinson's innocence and supported their father's defense of him.

"Why then," I asked, "do you think that these particular children in the novel were not prejudiced when most of their neighbors and school friends were?" Subsequently, most agreed that it had to do with the children's father and upbringing. I prompted their circle discussions with questions such as "Have you ever been discriminated against?" "If so, when and why?" The obvious responses of color, nationality, and religion surfaced. When I suggested they write whatever they did not feel comfortable talking about, other responses started to trickle in.

"Some people don't like me on their team, I'm kind of slow when I run."

"Some kids say I'm ugly, my brothers do too. When they have their camera in school they don't want me in the pictures."

"Some of my friends make fun of me cause I go to LD [learning disabilities] classes. They think I'm dumb and don't want me on their science team."

Kathy, a child of White South American and Black Caribbean heritage, usually sat inert and despondent during class discussions about racial issues. No matter what type of peer pressure was exerted, she refused to comment and countered the group's questions with stony silence and hostile glares. She also wrote journal entries that carefully skirted the issue of racism, but concentrated frequently on injustice. It wasn't until I asked for this writing that I was to find out the source of Kathy's misery:

> My aunt had all the family over for Easter a few years ago. When it came time to take pictures of the kids with their baskets, she asked me, my brother and my sister to step out of the way. She don't like my dad 'cause he's Black. I guess she don't like us 'cause we're not White. My cousins on my dad's side say he had to marry my mom. They make fun of me too. My mom's always depressed. My stupid sister is going with a White boy. I guess I don't ever feel like if I'm going to fit anywhere, and it's not my fault. It's not fair.

"I can't be part of their group," another student wrote. "Everything they do costs money. My parents can't just hand over money for the movies or the mall. So I make believe I'm not interested in their activities. They'd make fun of me if they thought I was poor. My mom and dad would kill me if I said to someone we had to count our money twice before spending it. No one in this neighborhood is supposed to be poor."

Another student who has an Asian father and a White mother tells me, "My mom acts real cool when I have my friends come over. She even drives them home. But afterwards she says, 'Why don't you have more White friends from our own neighborhood?'"

It surprised me that this particular student checked "White" on his high school application form. I never had the courage to ask him why. Later that semester, I proofread a description of himself in a letter he wrote to a prospective mentor. He stated that he looks "slightly Asian."

I read the students' comments and saw the ugly shreds of our social fabric that are woven into their personal lives and that destroy their self-confidence. That day I saw my students as vulnerable children, carrying on their shoulders the ills of our civilized world.

The class concluded the novel with new insight and raw feelings. The general consensus was that people are taught to be prejudiced and that racism and injustice have their roots in the home. Our frank discussions and open writing, I think, helped them air some of their previously hidden feelings and helped them begin to separate their opinions from those of their parents. Some of the students told me about a commercial that they had seen on television. In it, the first scene is of bassinets with newborns of different ethnic origins. Then the camera fades into a panorama of a graveyard. The narrator at this point says: "In our world, these shouldn't be the only two places where people don't care who's next door. Stop racism now." The students continued to worry, however, that there really were few cures. To quote Kathy, "Words are cheap. Actions come too late after the hurt has been done."

I asked the children to explain if affirmative action and civil rights have helped ease the division of the races. All agreed they had to a great extent, but that there is still much to accomplish. Most concluded, however, that they were just kids and were subjected to following rules and not making them. They had no choice but to accept the fact that their parents and the adults in their lives constantly exposed them to preconceived beliefs about racism and prejudice.

One journal entry states: "It is not easy to tell my dad not to call some of my friends Spics. He's my dad. He gets mad when I tell him not to say things like that. He's the boss. What he says goes."

I knew that I would never be able to answer their questions, or assuage their fears. Their pain was real and intense. They were hesitant to drop the issue, and I was terrified to continue. Yet I wanted this decision to be their call. I felt as if I no longer was directing the orchestra, but that the music was directing us.

The next novel I had in mind, Mildred Taylor's *Roll of Thunder, Hear My Cry*, was a mirror image of *To Kill a Mockingbird*. It was set at approximately the same time and also dealt with racial conflicts. *Roll of Thunder*, however, presents the racial conflict from the point of view of a Black child subjected to the horrors of racism in the South during the Depression, not from the point of view of White children. Taylor is a wonderful children's writer and her stories reflect the realism of an historical perspective. I proceeded with the same selection process as before, only this time the students immediately voted unanimously in favor of reading *Roll of Thunder*.

Again we started the literature circles by redefining the words *prejudice* and *racism*. This time the students' answers were not so hostile, not so combustible. I think the initial shock and reaction of talking about something that's always present, yet avoided, had worn off. They logically concluded, in one circle, that prejudice "is the result of preconceived judgments dictated by certain behaviors in the home and society." I was not only impressed, I was proud.

Issues of discrimination again surfaced, catapulted by certain issues in the novel. One of these issues surfaced when the Black children in the novel received used textbooks from the White schools; the textbooks were tattered and torn. One of the Black children in the story questioned why they had to learn from these old used-up books. We learned that it was the accepted practice in the South to give unusable materials to the "Nigra" schools. This fact brought on a new discussion of the "separate but equal" ruling.

We researched and examined the *Brown v. Board of Education* case and dissected and discarded the separate-but-equal practice as a Band-Aid cure for a social malignancy. We reviewed and applauded Rosa Parks's courageous and nonviolent stand against bigoted laws.

Some children asked older relatives if they remembered the "Whites Only" drinking fountains and rest rooms. Recollections of these times lived by grandparents and great-aunts were the topic of discussion for the entire morning. Horror stories of midnight lynchings and cross burnings were told again and again. Allen told a story he had heard about a neighbor of his great-aunt's in Mississippi who had been set on fire for supposedly stealing something from a White man's field. Allen's story made *Roll of Thunder* more real, more atrocious.

One part of the novel graphically describes the physical condition of a Black man set on fire by a posse of Klan members because he had allegedly looked at a White woman with a "degree of undisguised lust." The students compared this incident with Tom Robinson's trial in *To Kill a Mockingbird*. The circumstances and outcomes were similar, but as Allen put it, "Robinson had a White lawyer protecting him. It did nothing but buy him some time. This guy here had nothing but his words, and a Black man's word ain't worth nothing."

Nancy continued, "He was set on fire to set an example and make others afraid. I'm sure that if they wanted him dead they would have lynched him in the woods. They needed to send a message to the other Black folk that this could also happen to you. They had to spread fear, to intimidate."

All my students were disturbed by the fact that the Black children in the novel were expected to walk miles each day to school, while daily they were passed by a bus full of White kids going in the same direction. Their walks to school included being the object of humiliation as the White bus driver tried to run the children off the road and into muddy embankments.

At this point I asked the students to try to identify the improvements that they felt have occurred in public education since that time. I asked them how they would try to insure that all children received a similarly effective public education. The majority of their answers revolved around the need for the improvement of school facilities and the communities that surround them. Busing and integration, however, were the issues that reopened the proverbial can of worms. I was once again faced with an explosive issue with my classroom of both bused and neighborhood kids.

"Now minorities can get into colleges and jobs first just because of what they are." Shelly spoke without malice. The bused students, I detected, took offense at her statement.

"And if they are the token, they better watch their back, and they got to work twice as hard as their White peers." Nancy's words were spat out like rounds from a machine gun. Their target was obvious. Shelly seemed to gear up for another confrontation.

"Whites are just trying to play catch-up for all the years of inequality. They owe us." Kathy reasoned out loud, before Shelly could answer.

Larry commented next, "Who's kidding who? Yeah, so we come to this nice clean school in a White neighborhood. Who are the ones standing on a street corner in the early morning, in the rain and the snow and in the cold to catch the bus while most of the kids from around here are still in bed? You ever heard of a White kid being bused to our neighborhood? The Whites gave us rides to school all right, away from our own. Every time we try to get a piece of what the Whites got, it backfires on us. They fix it so we are pissed, and then they can say, 'Hey, ain't this what you wanted?' We always gonna be wrong, no matter what we get."

All the bused kids nodded their heads in agreement with Larry's comment. Not one of them had been spared the frustration of waiting for late buses during inclement weather.

Allen spoke slowly, deliberately, "Yeah, we come here and see all the stuff our neighborhood ain't. It's just like the textbooks that the Black kids got in the book. Our neighborhood's like that. We get the leftovers, the areas no one else wants."

I asked the group, "Do you feel that the environment here or the environment of your home school is more comfortable for you?" I wanted them to be specific, and I wanted substantiated answers. I did not want the class discussion to turn into an "Oh I'm so grateful I'm here" testimony. I asked the class to name specific examples of the pros and cons of busing, on the students' being bused and on the schools' receiving them. As I expected, the cons outweighed the pros. Some of the most indisputable reasons were the following:

"All our neighborhood friends are scattered all over. We all go to different receiving schools. The kids from here stay together. They grow together."

"I leave this place at 3:15, so I guess this place is integrated from 9:00 to 3:15, Monday to Friday, September to June, excluding all holidays."

"If the neighborhood kids want to stay for the after school programs and social center, they just walk back to school. If we want to stay we need an act of Congress, a way to get home after dark, a White family that will take us home with them until the activities start and three notes from our momma. It ain't worth all that."

"It is fine if one of the neighborhood kids learns to speak Spanish. Wow, how smart! How intelligent! But we're expected to learn English. Our Spanish ain't so smart. If we don't learn to speak like them, we're dumb."

One of the neighborhood kids asked if the bused kids felt just a little safer here, rather than in their neighborhood schools.

"Sure, but you better run like hell when those buses let you off in front of the home school. Then we got to walk the rest of the way to our house. Sometimes the gangs are there waiting for us to beat us up. At times it's like we're delivered right to them. It ain't all the time but it happens often enough."

The issues they mentioned as pros were touching:

"I've made some good friends."

"I see the kind of neighborhood I want my kids to grow in."

"I met Mrs. Gemmati."

"We do stuff like this—reading novels that kids in other schools don't do. We kinda have a say in things here."

One neighborhood student spoke up. "We don't have it all so great here. Some of the kids from this neighborhood that go to private schools won't talk to us because we talk to you."

Another neighborhood kid continued. "Yeah, they chase us and throw rocks at us, and if we are caught around their house, they try to beat us up because we go to this school. Because there's minorities at this school."

"The people around here don't care how good you are or what you do, and it ain't only the kids; they'd hate Mrs. Gemmati too because she's Puerto Rican."

The moment this was said, a hush permeated the classroom. All eyes turned toward me. I tried to remain unfazed but I felt yanked out of my neutral zone. I now was categorized, labeled, seen differently. I was no longer just the teacher. I was now one of the "sides" I had so desperately tried to stay out of. I hoped that this was the wedge necessary for me to help them realize that they needed to look at a person's qualities first and foremost.

I tried to ask for reasons for their persecution other than being members of our school. None were offered. The bused kids promised to help the neighborhood kids "show these bigots a lesson." I saw a subtle change in the kids toward the end of that particular discussion. I saw them bond, if only temporarily, against a common enemy.

The theme of inequality again was analyzed and cast as a result of racial prejudice. They discussed the fact that in *Roll of Thunder*, Cassie's family was targeted more than others because they had the distinction of being landowners. The students arrived at the conclusion that the Whites were uncomfortable with Blacks who had the potential for material equality—especially as landowners. Ultimately, at the end of the book, the students felt torn. They realized that Cassie's father had deliberately set his crop on fire to distract and ultimately stop the lynching of a neighbor's son. They knew that this crop was the only thing the family counted on to pay the taxes on their land. The students concluded that the family would either have to sell part of their land or lose it outright. They also knew that the boy who was saved from the lynching would now stand trial for the murder of a White man and would be convicted because of the improbability of a fair trial due to his color.

The children had a hard time dealing with the author's decision at this juncture. They compared the ending of *To Kill a Mockingbird* to this one and agreed that it was possible in *Roll of Thunder* for the Black family to keep the land their White neighbors so desperately wanted. "Their decision was a poor one," most maintained. "The kid couldn't be saved anyhow. What was the point?"

"Cassie's dad was faced with choosing between his beliefs and convictions, and the land that had been his since birth. He chose what he believed in," I announced quietly.

"Is that what you want from us, Mrs. Gemmati?"

"What's that?" I asked Shelly.

"You know, to let go of the stuff we see at home and make up our own minds about prejudice?"

Shelly's assumption took me by surprise. I literally had no idea that this was what I had unknowingly conveyed. I smiled at this group of students that I loved unconditionally.

"No," I responded. "What I want is not the issue. It's what you feel is right that's important. If I ask you to follow my convictions, I am doing no better than the person who tells you to believe that all Blacks are bad, that all Whites are racists or that all Hispanics are ignorant and loud. I strongly believe that the way to end prejudice is to stop taking another's judgment as your own. Don't let someone else prejudge for you."

The abrupt ending to the novel left them wanting answers and solutions to the problems we discussed. The novel tied no loose ends.

I attempted to explain that society's ills nowadays were the same yet different. One of the kids brought up the case of the Rodney King beating, and the subsequent beating of the truck driver during the ensuing riots in Los Angeles. Another student brought up the Jeffrey Dahmer case. All his victims were minorities.

"I wonder if the police would have returned that last Asian boy to Dahmer if the kid was White and Dahmer was the minority." Larry's comment surprised everyone.

An animated discussion on many "what ifs" followed. I sat back and listened. Their logic was, I thought, beyond their years.

My eighth graders have read their novels. The discussions, writings, and responses to literature in the format I established for the research dramatically changed our class.

Our feelings are still somewhat coarse, our nerves still exposed. These kids no longer tiptoe around issues of race. In many cases, the issue of race became the stated reason for even the most inconsequential verbal exchanges. Unfortunately, the following type of conversation became quite common in our classroom:

"Let me have a pen."

"Don't have another one."

"You won't let me have one 'cause I'm White. You think I should have my own pen. If I were Black, you'd lend me one. You're a racist."

"I don't care what color you are, girlfriend, I ain't got another pen."

"Why," I asked Nancy's literature circle a few days later, "haven't you ever discussed how these racial differences bothered you before?"

"They always were there, Mrs. Gemmati," she answered, "we just never acted on what we thought."

"Explain."

"It's like how do you act in church? Or in a library? Or when your mamma has company over? You don't act the same as when someone's there watching you, or when you're home and your mamma ain't there."

I knew exactly what she meant. I've become very sensitive about bringing up issues in class that could eventually lead to further rifts among what I once thought was a close-knit group of kids. Ignorance seems to be bliss and safe, but can I truly affect the lives of my students by reciting prerehearsed lines on a make-believe stage? Do I want to defer these discussions of race and prejudice to dark alleys that are constantly punctuated by the sound of gunfire? Do I let the neighborhood children continue to be steeped in the smog of superiority that is so choking and prevalent? It was an armor of racism that my students had been dressed in during their years of upbringing, one that was difficult to dent. I did find clues, hints maybe, that the confusion, frustration, and ordeal of adolescence was bleeding into another issue—the questioning of their parents' beliefs about different nationalities, races, and religions. As the year progressed, they wrote in their journals:

"I don't know how long he's (Dad's) felt that way [about others], but lots of things he grew up with ain't even around anymore. The movies ain't a dollar, and damn ain't considered a swear word."

"So what if I bring home someone who isn't Black. If that person loves me and respects me and doesn't do me wrong, why should I refuse him for a Brother who sells on the corner and is a player?"

"Why does she (Mom) call them rag heads? God, that pisses me off. How would she of felt if her Jewish grandfather married another Jew instead of her grandma? She isn't the puritanical Protestant she acts on Sunday all the rest of the week."

"I don't care if my dad says we have to stick to our own. If someone doesn't try to move into more decent places and show other people we ain't the loud and dirty Spics they say we are, how are they going to know different? Someone has to cross over to other neighborhoods and show that we want the same things they do."

The year was ending and I still did not feel closure with my students on these issues of prejudice. Their attitudes were shifting but their sense of one another was still fragile. I believed that the children felt this way too.

We were slated to go on the eighth grade school trip to Washington, and after our difficult year, the trip began to seem more of a necessity than an option. A few days away from school, parents, teachers, books, and students in other grades seemed like the perfect cure for what felt like a nagging cough. I figured if we didn't bond after being on a bus for umpteen hours and sharing sleeping quarters, there would be no hope.

Interestingly, the tension seemed to dissipate the farther we got from Chicago. As some kids dozed off, others left their groups to form new ones with those who remained awake. We talked about everything and nothing. The boundaries that identified us as people from specific places and with distinct roles got fuzzier and fuzzier. By the time we reached Philadelphia, we seemed to be one group of people, from Chicago, eager to spend uncurfewed time with one another. We cared about each other's luggage, comfort, and likes. We cared.

The tours of Washington were important, yes, and of course educational. But what I was looking at was more than the monuments that mark our country's growth. I was seeing in my students the behavior that is displayed when children are allowed to follow their basic friendly instincts—without worrying about approval or criticisms of who they speak to or who they hang around with.

On the last night before our long bus ride back to Chicago, my student teacher came banging on my door late at night. She was on the verge of hysteria, and it was a good long minute before she could inform me that a group of the kids had not returned to their rooms yet. She had fallen asleep and some of the kids had sneaked out. Just as I was about to dial the hotel security, Melissa ran into my room yelling that Nancy wouldn't answer the door, no matter how hard she banged on it. I dropped the phone and hurried down the hall. I yelled, I screamed, I kicked, but no one answered the door. I had my student teacher run down to the lobby to get a master key. I shuddered as the security guard opened the door.

The scene inside the room was incredible. Pop cans and popcorn were scattered everywhere, the TV was blaring, and about 15 of my students were asleep fully clothed, minus their shoes, which were piled up in a corner, fermenting. The kids were in an array of sleeping positions. Multicolored legs and arms were tangled everywhere. Nancy slowly opened her eyes and saw Shelly, Larry, Joe, and Maria sleeping on the same bed she had happened to crash on. Slowly they started to waken. They looked around and seemed surprised to find themselves in such a noisy, overcrowded room, with their teacher and a security guard standing in the doorway. I started laughing.

Freddy took one look at my faded Garfield sleeping shirt, my one sockless foot and tangle of hair and he started laughing. Pretty soon everyone was giggling at someone's sock, pointing at whomever with their thumb in their mouth, the drool coming from a half-open mouth, the weird look of half-closed eyes or disheveled hair.

The security guard looked at us as if we were truly nuts. "These your kids, Miss?"

"Yep," I answered. "Each and every one of them."

I would be lying to myself if I pretended to be the teacher I was before I had initiated this project. If anything, this research has taught me that hard talk on candid issues can take place within the safety of classroom walls. I know that a society that is free of prejudice is many, many years away, but it's something I hope to keep striving for—even if it's only in the microcosm of life that constitutes my classroom.

9 Teaching English Across the Technology/Wealth Gap

Charles Moran and Cynthia L. Selfe

In this article, we make three related points—each of which it pains us to recognize. The first is that, when we bring technology into our schools, we may be illuminating, and perhaps exacerbating, the advantage that students from wealthy families have over students who are less fortunate. Second, when we bring technology into our schools, we inevitably push something else out: Technology is expensive to buy, maintain, and learn to use. Third, when we bring technology into our schools, we need to understand that we may be fulfilling not only our goals for our students' learning, but also the commercial and political goals of those who have their own interests, not those of our students, at heart. And if these facts are hard for us to face as English language arts educators, they are also necessary focal points for our professional attention—as we prepare to enter the coming century at the end of this year, and as we prepare to enter our own classrooms and schools tomorrow morning.

Facing the Hard Facts about Technology Use in English Language Arts Classrooms

The Gap between Rich and Poor

Emerging technologies make visible, and perhaps increase, the gap between rich and poor and the related gap between races in this country. Here is a sad fact: In our educational system, and in the culture that this system

Reprinted from *English Journal,* July 1999.

reflects, computers *continue to be distributed differentially along the related axes of race and socioeconomic status,* and this distribution contributes to ongoing patterns of racism and to the continuation of poverty.

Schools primarily serving students of color and poor students continue to have less access to computers or access to less sophisticated computer equipment than do schools primarily serving more affluent and white students. Similarly, these schools have less access to the Internet, to multimedia equipment, to CD-ROM equipment, to local area networks, and to videodisc technology than do schools primarily serving more affluent and white students (Coley, Crandler, & Engle 3). Poor families in both urban and rural environments and black and Hispanic Americans are much less likely to own and use computers than individuals with higher family incomes and white families (*Getting America's Students Ready* 36). In other words, the poorer students and their families are—and in this country wealth is highly correlated with race—the less likely they are to have access to computers and, later, the less likely they are to gain access to high-paying, high-tech jobs in the American workplace.

As English language arts teachers, we have always understood that some students in our classes come from relatively wealthy homes and others come from relatively poor homes—and that these facts shape their literacy skills and experiences. Some students have homes with desks and the privacy that permits reading and writing; others move from apartment to apartment and have no place to do their homework. Some of our students get allowances, and some work after school to help their families pay the bills. Despite the fact that wealth in this country is a function of both race and class, we have come to accept these differences as just the way things are. As writing teachers, we have worked to level the playing field, bringing in pencils and paper for those who needed the writing instruments of that time.

Now that computers are the writing instrument of choice, however, we are likely to receive in a given set of student essays a few pieces that are beautifully formatted and desktop-published, incorporating Web research and images. In the same set, we are also likely to receive a few pieces that are handwritten on ruled paper, with messy-looking erasures, layers of correction fluid, or simply crossed out errors. Of course, we are talking about appearance here, but we're also talking about speed and ease of composition, revision, editing, and research. As one of us wrote sixteen years ago in this journal, "most writers who have access to word-processing machinery use it" (Moran 113). What was true in 1983 is true today. Most writers who have access to technology make full use of computers in their writing and research. Students with access to this technology at home and at school have an edge—just as do students with access to good nutrition, homework space, and medical care. Technology illuminates and exacerbates the wealth gap—a gap that, as economists agree, is rapidly widening in this country and around the globe (Castells, Krugman, Thurow, US Bureau of Census).

The Cost of Technology

As we recognize the technology gap that divides our students, both one from another and district from district, educators quite properly try to level the playing field by becoming the students' technology provider of last resort. And here is where we get ourselves in trouble, bringing us to our second point—that technology is, simply put, extremely expensive, and that when we lobby for technology in our schools, we are implicitly lobbying for the removal of something else. To equip a writer with a pencil and paper costs a dime, or at most two. To equip that same writer with a fully equipped and supported writing facility costs thousands of dollars. Studies reported in *Scientific American* tell us that it costs a corporation $13,000 a year to own a PC (Gibbs 87). The cost is composed of depreciation of the hardware and software (30 percent a year), hardware support, software support, training, and the time the users spend learning how to make the machine do what they want it to do.

From our experience in public schools and colleges, we believe that the costs associated with technology in industry are comparable to the costs experienced by educational institutions. If so, it follows that if we want to integrate emerging technologies into our teaching and our students' learning, we should expect to spend $13,000 per workstation per year. Should we spend less than industry finds it must spend, then we'll cut out classroom support, instructional assistance, and professional development, and we'll find ourselves frustrated and confused, likely to recreate the scene that we so often see in schools: computers sitting unused, and often unusable, in labs, classrooms, and supply closets; teachers who want to try using technology resources, but who don't have the time, the training, or the resources to do so. So if we want to use technology in ways that work well for both teachers and students, and if we want to bring, let us say, one hundred computer workstations into our high school building, we should add an item of $1,300,000 to our school budget—an *annual* item, not a one-time cost. And we'll have to find that $1,300,000 somewhere. Increased property taxes in the district? Not likely, in our present antitax frame of mind. If additional taxes are not available, then the money will have to be found within the existing school budget, which means that something substantial gets cut. Building maintenance? A few faculty lines and the resultant larger classes? Art and music? Languages other than English? The trade-off for a school that spends $3,000 per student per year will be more painful and destructive than the trade-off for a school that spends $6,000 per student per year, but in both cases something substantial will be lost. And what will be the gain?

In some states, legislators and/or voters have put forward technology-funding initiatives that seem to solve the problem by adding new money. But these initiatives seem always to be coupled with cuts in other spending for education, so that at the end of the process there has been a painful, destructive trade-off. As Todd Oppenheimer writes:

> New Jersey cut state aid to a number of school districts this past year and then spent $10 million on classroom computers. In Union City, California, a single school district is spending $27 million to buy new gear for a mere eleven schools . . . in Mansfield, Massachusetts, administrators dropped proposed teaching positions in art, music, and physical education, and then spent $333,000 on computers. (46)

Hidden Agendas

This brings us to our final point: Advocates for technology often have an agenda that has nothing to do with our students' learning. If one is a politician or academic administrator in this decade, it is almost mandatory to call for technology in our schools, not because of any proven link between technology and learning—there is really no consistent evidence of such a link, especially in language arts and literacy studies—but because technology is seen as a potential quick and cheap fix for the perceived problems in our educational system. Anything associated with technology has a special glow these days. We note in this regard the extraordinary bubble in technology stocks that is helping to drive the stock market. This technology-effect accounts in a substantial degree for our present administration's drive to bring the Internet to every school in the country. We refer all teachers to the widely-cited 1996 report from the US Department of Education, *Getting America's Students Ready for the 21st Century: Meeting the Technology Literacy Challenge, A Report to the Nation on Technology and Education*. This report is based on President Clinton's statement that "we know, purely and simply, that every single child must have access to a computer . . ." (4). Estimates indicate that this national project to expand technological literacy may cost up to $109 billion—averaging either $11 billion annually for a decade or between $10 and $20 billion annually for five years—from a variety of sources at the national, state, and local levels (*Getting America's Students Ready* 5). In comparison to the federal funding this country is allocating to other literacy and education projects, these amounts stagger the imagination. To put these expenditures for technology into perspective, we can look at the 1999 budget for the Department of Education that President Clinton recently sent to the United States Congress. In this budget, the President has requested $721 million of direct federal funding for educational technology; but less than half of that amount, $260 million, for the America Reads Challenge; and less than one-tenth of that amount, $67 million, for teacher recruitment and preparation ("Community Update" 3).

Taking Steps to Make Change with Technology

"OK, OK," we hear you say. "Enough! We see the inequities, we see that the gap is widening, we see that access to technology, and everything else that money can buy, is increasingly unequal. We see that our political leaders are feeding the techno-hype that makes us, and our students, and their parents and guardians, nervous unless we spend more of our diminishing school resources on expensive high-tech. What should we do?" While answers are never as easy as questions, we have a few thoughts.

We need to remain sensitive to what is happening with the distribution of wealth in our country, and we need to bring up this wealth gap and its relation to race whenever we can in conversations with colleagues and friends and with our students in class discussions. Given the increasing wealth gap, do we really want more tax cuts for the wealthy? Do the fabled "Welfare Cadillacs" consume more of the nation's resources than the white-collar crime that led to the savings-and-loan bailout? The wealth gap might become part of our curriculum—instead of presenting our economy as booming, we could note the wealth gap and inquire into its likely social consequences. We might, for example, ask students to compare the technology resources and budgets of schools in different districts, different parts of town, different parts of the world—comparing the distribution and use of technology resources in rich and poor districts, in the homes of rich and poor students, in first and third world countries. Or we might have students read Cathy Camper's "A Note from the Future" from *Wired* magazine. (See Appendix.)

Let's use what we know, perhaps not to bring about the revolution, but to bring about the awareness that makes change possible. Let's read, too, Berliner and Biddle's *The Manufactured Crisis* and understand that our educational system is pretty good and does not need to see technology as its last, best hope. There's no reason to panic.

In our professional organizations—in the NCTE and the IRA—we need to recognize that if written language and literacy practices are our professional business, so is technology. This recognition demands a series of carefully considered and very visible professional stands on a variety of technological issues now under debate in this country: on the access issues we have discussed, on the issue of technology funding for schools, on the issue of multiple venues for students' literacy practices, on the national project to expand technological literacy, and so on. We need to engage in much more of this kind of professional activism, and more consistently.

But at the same time that we recognize the connections between literacy and technology, we have to keep our priorities straight, focusing on education and making sure that technology is following the principles we hold central as teachers, not leading or distorting them. Seymour Papert, in *Mindstorms*, recommended intensive computer use for K–12 students. In Papert's plan, students would program computers, using the language LOGO, and would thereby learn writing, logic, processes and procedures, velocities, rates of change, spatial and algebraic relationships—indeed most of what we think we should be teaching in school.

As a responsible educator, Papert had to deal with the issues of cost and access. He did so by assuming that students would own their computers for thirteen years—an assumption that Microsoft and others in the hardware/software industry have recently made to seem downright foolish. These commercial vendors try to convince us that we need to be on the cutting edge, MMX-capable, with hard drives filled with the latest software. Computers are obsolete after four years, we are told—by marketing campaigns directed by CEOs who are themselves receiving immense salaries. Such marketing strategies inevitably shape the thinking of parents and guardians, who in the face of the increasing wealth gap are afraid that depriving their children of cutting-edge technologies now will similarly affect their prospects for prosperity and success after graduation.

Papert was thinking not of technology, but of education. His LOGO curriculum was designed around strategies for effective teaching and learning—active inquiry, hands-on practice, engaging problem solving. It was not designed as the latest installation of high technology. He was right:

For his LOGO curriculum, the same computer would last for thirteen years, for the full extent of the student's K–12 education. Its cost, therefore, could be prorated over these thirteen years and would be a cost, certainly, but one that, he argued, was 5 percent of the total spending on a student's K–12 education.

Keeping up with the dangers of technology and the ways in which we need to revalue our old Apple IIs, IBM 286s, and Mac Classics is equally important. These machines—now in garages and attics—are often entirely usable as writing instruments in certain situations and for certain assignments. Even our 286s were, and would still be, fine for e-mail and for Lynx-access. As writers, do we *always* need cutting-edge technologies? As Michael Levy has noted, "In the twentieth century, it takes a special kind of courage to continue to use a particular technology once it is considered to be outmoded, even if that technology is more than adequate for the task at hand" (2). What we and our students get as writers from our supercharged PCs is not always necessary, unless we are working seriously with composition in multimedia environments. And often in such environments, unless we plan assignments carefully, the only skill we provide students using cutting-edge workstations is the ability to find, in color, with graphics and animation, commercial advertising.

So, as educators, maybe we can think—at least on an occasional basis— more about how to create increasingly effective teaching and learning opportunities with the technology we already have than about how to stay up with the very latest technology. If we were to take this direction, we'd want to say that we were educators first and technology-lovers second. We'd need to be strong enough to seem a little backward, to resist the marketing hype that we've so readily fallen for, our acceptance of the belief that schools are doing a bad job (they are not) and that technology is the way to turn things around (it is not). On the other hand, we'd be ready for the world's discovery, forecast by Todd Oppenheimer in the Atlantic, that the investment we've been making in computerizing our schools has not paid off; or its discovery, outlined by Gibbs in Scientific American, that over the past decade, companies/industries that have made the greatest investment in information technologies have had the slowest growth.

We can work locally, and constructively, with the low-end technology that is out there, an underground technology that gets very little press because there's not enough profit in it. Low-cost word-processors like Alpha SmartBoards—laptops that cost approximately $200, run for sixty hours on rechargeable penlight batteries, and hold one hundred pages of text—are just fine for many writing tasks. Students can compose on these word-processors and, when they need to print, can go to a PC print station and upload their file. There's no learning curve, and the boards are practically indestructible.

The Western Massachusetts Writing Project has acquired seventy such machines, which it lends to teachers for two- to three-month periods on the condition that the teachers integrate the technology into a project that effectively teaches. English language arts educators in this program find that both they and their students learn more about writing and publishing, and more about technology, than they have before, and at very low cost. True, even inexpensive word-processing machines do cost $200, which is still a whole lot more than the ten-cent pencil; and true, most students do not go home to computers. But this approach suggests that there are low-cost ways of integrating technology with curriculum. In schools that once saw themselves as poor, with faculty who once saw themselves as technophobes, we find teachers successfully lobbying their principals and superintendents for similar low-end machines for their classrooms (Hunter & Moran).

In language arts and English classrooms, we need to recognize that we can no longer simply educate students to become technology users—and consumers on autopilot—without also helping them learn how to understand technology issues from socially and politically informed perspectives. When English language arts faculty require students to use computers to complete a range of assignments—without also providing them the time and opportunity to explore the complex issues that surround technology and technology use in substantive ways—we may, without realizing it, be contributing to the education of citizens who are habituated to technology use but who have little critical awareness about, or understanding of, the complex relationships among humans and machines and the cultural contexts within which the two interact.

Composition teachers, language arts teachers, and other literacy specialists need to recognize that the relevance of technology in the English studies disciplines is not simply a matter of helping students work effectively with communication software and hardware, but, rather, also a matter of helping them understand and be able to assess—to pay attention to—how the social, economic, and pedagogical implications of new communication technologies and technological initiatives affect their lives. Knowledgeable literacy specialists at all levels need to develop age-appropriate and level-appropriate reading and writing activities aimed at this goal. This approach—which recognizes the complex links that now exist between

literacy and technology at the end of the twentieth century—constitutes a
critical technological literacy that will serve students well.

There are other suggestions we can think of. In districts, systems, and
states that have poor schools, rural schools, and schools with large
populations of students of color, we need to resist the forces that continue to
link technological literacy with patterns of racism and poverty. We need to
insist on and support more equitable distributions of technology.

In our voting for school board members, in committee meetings, in public
hearings, at national conventions, in the public relations statements of our
professional organizations, we have to argue—every chance we get—that
poor students and students of color get more access to computers and to
more sophisticated computers, that teachers in schools with high
populations of such students be given more support.

In preservice and inservice educational programs and curricula we need
to help all English language arts teachers get more education on both
technology use and technology criticism. In the curricula comprising our
own graduate programs and the educational programs that prepare teachers
for careers in our profession, we need to make sure these programs don't
simply teach young professionals to *use* computers—but rather, that we
teach them how to pay attention to technology and the issues that result
from, and contribute to, the technology-literacy linkage. It is no longer
enough, for instance, simply to ask preservice teachers to learn to use
computers for their English language arts classes. Instead, we need to help
them read in the areas of technology criticism, social theories, and computer
studies and then provide them with important opportunities to participate in
making hard decisions about how to pay attention to—and affect—
technology issues in departments, colleges, schools, and local communities;
how to address the existing links between literacy and technology in
curricula at all levels; how to provide more access to technology for more
people; and how to help individuals develop their own critical
consciousness about technological literacy.

In libraries, community centers, and other nontraditional public places,
literacy educators need to provide free access to computers for citizens at the
poverty level and citizens of color—not only so that such individuals can
become proficient in computer use for communication tasks (Oppel), but
also so that these citizens have access to the Internet and to online sites for
collective political action (Hoffman and Novak).

If we are on the horns of a national dilemma—caught between the
contending forces of technology and literacy, poverty and race—it is a dilemma

that is of our own making, one that we can unmake. We can, through individual and collective action, work against the patterns and trends we have delineated here. Indeed, we must. Our responsibility, our obligation as English language arts teachers—if we truly believe that education should provide equal opportunities for citizens in our country—is to pay attention and to act on behalf of students and the future they represent.

Works Cited

Berliner, David C., and Bruce J. Biddle. *The Manufactured Crisis: Myths, Fraud, and the Attack on America's Public Schools.* Reading, Massachusetts: Addison-Wesley, 1995.

Castells, Manuel. *End of Millennium,* Volume II of The Information Age, Economy, Society and Culture. Malden, MA: Blackwell Publishers, 1998.

Coley, R. J., J. Crandler, and P. Engle. *Computers and Classrooms: The Status of Technology in US Schools.* Educational Testing Service, Policy Information Center. Princeton, NJ: ETS, 1997.

"Community Update." *Newsletter of the US Department of Education.* Office of Intergovernmental and Interagency Affairs. 55 (March 1998) Washington, D.C.

Getting America's Students Ready for the 21st Century: Meeting the Technology Literacy Challenge, A Report to the Nation on Technology and Education. US Department of Education. Washington, D.C., 1996.

Gibbs, W. Wayt. "Taking Computers to Task." *Scientific American* 276.2 (July 1997): 82–89.

Hoffman, Donna L., and Thomas P. Novak. "Bridging the Racial Divide on the Internet." *Science 280* (17 April 1998): 390–91.

Hunter, Patricia F., and Charles Moran. "Writing Teachers, Schools, Access, and Change." *Literacy Theory in the Age of the Internet.* Eds. Todd Taylor and Irene Ward. New York: Columbia University Press, 1998: 158–69.

Krugman, Paul. *Peddling Prosperity: Economic Sense and Nonsense in the Age of Diminished Expectations.* New York: W. W. Norton, 1994.

Levy, Michael. *Computer-Assisted Language Learning: Context and Conceptualization.* New York: Oxford University Press, 1997.

Moran, Charles. "Word Processing and the Teaching of Writing." *English Journal* 72.3 (1983): 113–15.

Oppel, Shelby. "Computer Lab Offers Escape from Poverty." *The St. Petersburg Times* 17 September 1997: 3B.

Oppenheimer, Todd. "The Computer Delusion." *The Atlantic Monthly* 280.1 (1997): 45–62.

Papert, Seymour. *Mindstorms: Children, Computers, and Powerful Ideas.* New York: Basic Books, 1980.

Thurow, Lester. "Why Their World Might Crumble: How Much Inequality Can a Democracy Take?" *New York Times Magazine* 19 November 1995: 78–79.

US Bureau of the Census, Current Population Reports, Series P23–189. Population Profile of the United States: 1995. Washington, DC: US Government Printing Office, 1995.

APPENDIX

A Note from the Future

Passed on to *Wired* by Cathy Camper

In January of 1995 *Wired* published this letter in its *idées fortes* section. There was no introduction to it and no commentary following it. We could also find no letters from readers written to the magazine in response to it. As you read the letter, think of reasons *Wired* may have featured "A Note from the Future" in quite this way.

To the Onerabl Acadmy of Compvtr Siånses:

Bak then, sum histery boks long ago tim bak, think NOW be in the futvr. Sayin futvr babys har is all in mohaks. Or som pictErs showd rockits and we al on the mon. Big soots on an wakking jus lik sno. Or tak plastik. Sad axvaly we yoos it to wear clos.

HA HA Wish they cold truly see how futvr isrelly. Al rich foks plug in to a vertvl reelity Masheen, wich is lik wakin into a bilbord whats clean with a fotry goin on an peepl not sik but hapy in there NIS cartuon.

Now, spoz to rit a thim say why yo let me in scool for this contes yo hav. Why ho cum this scool be somethin lnrd. Lik you cant not see it in the way Irite. Like I wood got an equl chans with compvter joks, who can typ an go to scool longer than I new how to writ, svr Im svr, we get the same dog cor chans wenit cor cums to a job. Ha evan a dog no, shet on that.

How do yo think, see a sistim anlis job an I don evan no envf numers to pvnch in an git insid the dor? What kin of felings about microwaf clos drirs, on tv, or drivin cokit soler car or envf mony to pay my clen air bils, So Tri stats AIR compnis don cvttim me of evry month crs I don hef a job.

Yes, tru naf the worl be wakkin on air, be zoming on a computer scren, buzzin an evry dog cor thin jes lik olen tim books did say. But the other haf, they me, livin in the reel wrld twirl, wich you lef ames. Yes, we we rin plastik clos. But they slimmy 1970 poly eser from the yvsd clos stor. Yeh we vizoolizin reelity. But it a dvm karnty gaim for 25 sent. An they shet rong abot 1 thing. We not wenn any mohaks, in this futvr nov, We so cris dog col, we grow har lon jes kep us warm.

Probly I am what you cal colerd, as lik wity was the blank pags of a colering bok, An al the waksy flashy brite scribly outta lin stvf, that was us. Probly I am femal, probly I got no job An lotsA kids. Probly. But how yo gonna now? Im not plvgEd in, I am still a BodE. Some bodees tvk in Avtvvl reelity.

So I Ask yo plez, to red this wel An I hop I can be in yur skool. I do not ask to be a compvtr jok or a sistim anilis, but jes can I beter myself, An mAbe sAy envf my hvsband An me by A kid. Be sum kin of tru blv family be jvs lik the boks, only I ned axses to a compvtr soon, or to bad, I be loss an it will be to lat.

10 Writing to Think Critically: The Seeds of Social Action

Randy Bomer

Kendra is a student in a writing workshop, and she keeps a writers notebook so that writing can become a tool for thinking in her life. She has written about the day she saw a blue jay aggressively tossing twigs and leaves out of the gutter on her friend's apartment building; about her feelings regarding being on a soccer team that loses all its games; about her memories of each room in her grandmother's apartment. She has even written reflections on her life history as a reader. She has entries in her notebook about sunlight, icicles, and the early-morning sound of crows. Today, she writes about her ex-boyfriend, whom she makes a point of not naming, and how his jealousy whenever she talked to male friends made her break up with him.

When Kendra walks home from school, she may be thinking about any of these things. Or she may think about other things around her. She may think about the housing project she walks past and the friends who live there. She may think about the air she breathes, as she avoids the rear of buses because the exhaust makes her cough. Like many of the children in her neighborhood, she has asthma and so takes care, when possible, about what she breathes. She may notice the billboards advertising cigarettes on the sides of buildings. She sometimes thinks about the rumors she's heard about drugs being sold out of the building in front of which she always sees the same couple fighting. Usually, the man is yelling at the woman, but once she heard the woman scream back at the man, calling him a "faggot."

On her eight-block walk home, when she is out in the world, Kendra encounters dozens of sights, sounds, and interactions that could potentially

Reprinted from *Voices from the Middle,* May 1999.

speak of social injustice, exploitation, and risk. But none of these find their way into her writers notebook. "It just doesn't seem like they belong there," she says. Why would that be?

One of the goals many writing teachers share is that of enabling students, usually rendered voiceless in the world at large, to speak for social change in their writing. Many hope that students will feel empowered to make memos, letters, pamphlets, posters, speeches, agendas, and other texts that seek to address unfairness in society, that ask for redress, that call for public attention to problems and possibilities. We want students to view their writing as more than exercises for learning to write, as more than obedience to teacher instructions, but rather as a unique form of social action. In many of our classrooms, however, it has been hard to get this agenda rolling, except when the teacher sponsors it. Students seldom walk in the door of our classrooms sharing our vision of writing as social action, and the topics they choose, important to them though they may be, often seem socially static as *the topic I am writing about for English,* rather than as *the social agenda I am pursuing in the world.*

This is not a flaw in their thinking; they have learned well the lessons school has taught. We may not have done enough yet to disrupt their expectation that their work is nothing but compliance. It is ironic that so often, when they do write to address social issues, it is in obedient response to a teacher prompt. Wouldn't it be useful to teach them to develop their own topics and agendas for social action in response to the world they walk through every day? Perhaps a way to begin might involve attention to their use of writing as a tool for thinking. Since writers' notebooks have been so valuable for many of us in helping students develop the habits of mind that lead to the writing of poetry, memoir, fiction, essay, articles, and other writing, they might be useful, too, in bringing a socially critical lens to the lifework of writing.

Teaching writing as a tool for thinking, we teachers cannot help but emphasize certain kinds of thinking over others. For instance, in *Time for Meaning* (1995), I describe having students sit with one object they find in the room—a square of tile, a pencil, a shoe—for 10 minutes and write just about that one thing. In demonstrating this sustained attention, I usually describe the object in detail and sometimes think associatively off of it. In my way of teaching this lesson, I'm valuing observation and associative thinking. The other minilessons I describe for teaching a variety of ways to write in notebooks similarly underscore the value of particular ways of thinking and writing, including: a curiosity about people (a characterizing mode of thought), an ear for spoken language (a vocalizing thinking), a style of deep lingering in memory (reconstructive thought), a reflectiveness about current life events (interpretive thinking), a responsiveness to literature and other media (a dialogical habit of mind), and others. Sometimes, people mistake these for attempts to get at the writer's own, real, true, individual voice, but they are not. Really, they are modes of thinking that I'm setting up as values in the classroom community, the ways with words I'm trying to socialize the kids into. Of course, there is no way to be exhaustive in the kinds of thinking-with-writing one chooses to emphasize: there are always more possibilities excluded than included. But it's important to note that our choices create and constrain the reservoirs of possibility from which our students will draw, at least as long as they're in our classes.

Given the possibilities I introduce for writing in notebooks, it's not surprising that, when students reread their notebooks and construct a theme or topic on which to expand and create a piece for readers, they usually select topics about people, memory, reflections on current personal issues, and topics based on close observation of the material world around them. Rarely do they develop in their notebooks topics related to social issues, everyday justice, power relationships, possibilities for collective interest and action, or other topics I would think of as social, political, or critical. Sometimes, there could be a critical angle on the material they choose. Often, I, as a reader, see this potential because of the lenses I bring to their drafts. However, their ways of thinking about their topics, their ways of "writing well," usually remain more personal, poetic, and descriptive.

For example, when Sarai wrote in her notebook:

> The whole time I was little, my mother owned a candy store. I use to walk there after school. I could take a piece of candy and some-thing to read. As long as it wasn't to much. Then a bigger nice store opened up on the same block. My mother didn't have any customers and she had to close the store. Now she works in an office, but I never saw it.

That could have become a piece about the ways people with little, struggling businesses are defeated by bigger, richer companies. It could have dealt with themes of people trying to integrate families into work, sometimes possible in entrepreneurial venues, rarely possible in more bureaucratic contexts. Instead, when Sarai used this material as part of a larger memoir, it became a lovely, wistful description of those afternoons in her mother's store. As was almost always the case, the lens Sarai brought to her memory was not social, political, economic, justice-oriented, but rather private, personal, and aesthetic. Nothing was wrong with what she did; in fact, I liked it. But might she have thought and written about it differently—with different questions and purposes—if I had found a way to highlight more critical habits of mind in the notebook itself, the seedbed for their larger works?

After all, my own notebooks are full of critical reflections, a good deal more of those, in fact, than close observations of objects. So are the notebooks of many of my writing friends. Flipping through the last week or so of my notebook, I see notes from a workshop on feminist literature, followed by my response to the workshop in which I question whether the professor-presenter's self-aggrandizing subtext positioned the middle and high school teachers she was addressing in the same sort of oppression as the women experienced in the story she discussed. There is a narrative of a fireman from the station down the street rudely ordering workmen at my next-door neighbor's house to move their truck that was blocking his personal car, and my wondering about the tone of authority automatically lent by a uniform. One short entry notices a little girl asking her big brother, "Can I watch you play?" An entry I made while waiting to see a teacher describes in detail the physical appearance of the school's interior. Since it is a school in a poor neighborhood, nothing in it seems to be in clean or good condition. I remind myself to make a similar entry the next time I am in a corporate office, waiting to see a grants officer. There is, very often, a sort of second act to my thinking. There is the description of things that happen, but then there is a critique of it, usually through some sort of concern for the kind of society we should have. It is that second act I would like to bring to students' thinking in their notebooks.

Noticing in School

School, of course, is no more immune to the issues of justice, power, and association than any other human institution. Follow any student around for the day at school, and you will likely encounter:

- questions of fairness about how people get picked for jobs, teams, or groups;
- evidence of the low esteem in which school is held in society, including inadequate supplies and decrepit buildings;
- oppression of younger people by elders;
- the power relations that surround "respect" and "disrespect";

- complexities of how a group of people can get along together;
- decisions about how a group deals with an individual who will not conform;
- issues of voice and silence;
- abbreviated rights of free speech, free association, free press, and other Constitutional "guarantees";
- the relations between individual choices (of topics, inquiries, reading material) and shared community pursuits;
- the power relations encoded in language, e.g., "correct" usage and pronunciation;
- the consequences of cruelty and kindness;
- restrictions on being able to move freely among different groups (classes, small groups, friendship groups).

Every one of these issues is deeply political, and any event in which they could arise is an opportunity for students to think about political themes that are continually present in our lives at all levels, from home to the world at large. These are the same issues for which people go to prison, endure torture, and die. I am not here advocating a student revolution, anarchy in schools, or classrooms completely run by children's wishes. My point is that these sorts of topics are just as available in children's daily experiences as the frost on the windows or their trips to visit relatives. And since they are so close at hand, we make a political decision in helping students develop an attentive lens to notice them—or in failing to do so.

Subjects of study (other than writing) in school also present locations for critical questioning. Social studies obviously focuses on relevant topics, but science and math are not free of potential problems, either. Since most readers of this journal do their work in English/language arts, it might be most useful for us to glance at the ways a critical habit of mind can be fostered in the reading of literature. When we read literature, we transact with the sentences of a text in order to construct a virtual world. We collaborate with authors, and to some extent, we allow them to set up shop in our own thinking. Critical reading (and here I mean socially critical in a Freirean sense [Freire, 1992; Freire and Macedo, 1987], as I have throughout this essay, not literary-critical or critical of the quality of writing) demands that we interrogate the worlds we read with lenses similar to the ones we use to ask questions of the material world around us. Critical reading can foster thinking that can lead to social action, if we help readers learn to ask themselves questions like the following:

- Is this story fair?
- How does the purpose or point of this text address what people like me care about? ("People like me" are members of the same social groups.)
- How does this text address the perspectives of other groups, especially those who usually don't get to tell their side?
- How does this story make us think about justice in the world?
- What perspective is missing in this text (one that could be there)? What would it be like if we put it back?
- How does this story deal with individuals and groups? Are the people alone and in contests with each other, or does the story help us imagine people getting together?
- How does money work in this story?
- How different are people allowed to be in this story? Does it assume everyone's happy and good in the same ways?

Actively Teaching a Socially Critical Lens for Thinking

It's one thing to be aware of the possibility of notebook writing that focuses on social issues and questions, but the problem remains of how to teach students to do this sort of thinking and writing. In order to think through the craft of teaching something so intangible as a critical lens, it will help us to consider three modes of teaching: demonstration, assisted performance, and reflective conversation (Bomer, 1998).

Demonstration

I don't know how to assist students in learning to write in a particular way, or how to lead discussions about strategies and lenses, unless I am doing some of the same sort of writing myself. I can't buy examples of writers' notebooks shrink-wrapped with the lives from which they sprang: I have to use my own living, thinking, and writing as exemplars. A teacher's own writing not only lends credibility to the teaching: it also provides me with material for minilessons and conferences. Furthermore, my writing, full of local references, culturally familiar to the students, helps them see that social action inquiry is not out there somewhere, but is, rather, right here at hand.

Writing demonstrations can be of two kinds: after-the-fact and in-the-midst. In demonstrations after-the-fact, we read to the students our own notebook entries written outside of class, sometimes putting them on overheads or chart paper. The actual text of what we wrote, though, is only part of the story. We situate the text within a narrative of when and how we wrote it. Here is a rough sketch of the general idea:

> Yesterday, I was driving home from school, and I saw [this or that], and I started wondering about it. I was thinking about [blah-blah], and when I got home, here's what I wrote: [reading of text].

Depending upon the actual content, the minilesson would go on to describe what the students could learn from this example.

Demonstrations in-the-midst are perhaps even more useful because the noticing, thinking, and writing can all happen on the spot, right there where the students can see it. Choosing something out the window or in the room, or perhaps an event from the hallway during the passing period just before class, the teacher speaks aloud about her/his wondering and reflecting for a minute or so, then decides aloud how to write this thinking, and begins composing in front of the students on an overhead or chart paper. It is, after all, not self-evident how to start such an entry. Does one first write a description of what one saw, or does one begin with the larger critical issue that is now beginning to take shape? How does one start writing about a big idea? There's no right answer, but the decision, one that some writers find paralyzing, has to be made, and no other mode of teaching can even get close to that level of detail.

Assisted Performance

To bridge from our own doing to students' activity, it is useful to provide structured assistance, chances for them to try out these strategies and lenses with our help. As is the case with most major advances in students' habits of thinking and writing, even as students begin to attempt to work independently, they also need our help. Even strong students may have trouble adopting a critical lens, sometimes because the very same compliant, uncomplaining nature that has made them successful in school also makes them reticent about detecting problems in their social worlds. Whole-class assisted performance allows the teacher to begin inducting students into the desired way of seeing. After a shared event, like yesterday's pep rally or assembly, a disturbance in the hall today, or a field trip, it's useful to spend first a few minutes of a minilesson orally constructing critical questions and perspectives, then asking students to write to extend their thinking, then asking them to discuss with a partner the angle they adopted in their notebook entry. Taking a walk together around the neighborhood, or even just around the campus, provides a chance to focus everyone's attention on critical reflection if the walk is followed up with time for writing and discussion. Photography and videotape provide media for bringing the world into the classroom. Taped news segments, short excerpts of shows, and student- or teacher-produced images of provocative scenes from the world can help students tune their attention to areas of experience they might not yet have considered. These whole-class strategies, which early on might need more than a minilesson to complete in any satisfying way, provide support for the large group to catch on to the intellectual process we are setting in motion in the class.

Of course, in a writing workshop, much assisted performance occurs in teacher conferences with individual students. Often, in writers' notebooks, students have summarized events without doing much critical reflection about them. A helpful conference, in such a case, is a collaborative conversation that brings out the potential political themes in the event and leaves the student writing into that same sort of thinking.

Early student attempts at being critical often tend to be over-simplified opinions or complaints, rather than a more complex analysis of a social problem. In conference with writers at that stage of development, the teacher helps the student consider the problem from multiple perspectives, not in order to crush the writer's own view, but to allow the issue to develop more facets. When a student has begun to develop a catalogue of social ills, a useful conference may involve imagining together possible alternatives or remedies to the problem, especially planning the ways one could, by gathering other people together around the concern, begin working to make it better. As some of these conferences become successful, these same writers, by sharing with the class what they have learned, can provide a demonstration for others.

Reflective Conversation

Regular appointments in which students are asked to give an account of how they have been working toward heightened awareness of social issues in their writing help to keep student attention focused on the goal. If I know that, at the end of today's writing time, I'm going to have to write a note, talk to a partner, or report to the class about what I've been trying to do in my critical writing-to-think, I'm more likely to make sure my work gives me something valuable to say. Simple questions can begin complex discussions:

- What kinds of topics do you notice yourself getting passionate about?
- What is giving you trouble about this kind of thinking?
- If you were going to teach someone to do the kind of writing we've been working on, what would be important to tell them?
- Which strategies have you tried so far in your notebook, and which ones do you need to work on?
- Who tried something new today?
- What topics have you already written about that you want to write more about?
- What are we learning at this point?

Such conversations are more than share sessions. They help the teacher monitor students' constructs. They allow students to self-assess and name their own thinking and learning. They represent the community's ongoing collaboration toward the values informing this work.

Rereading for Themes and Possibilities

Once students have at least ten notebook entries focused on social issues, noticings, and questions, they should be able to reread their notebooks for themes. The question with which they read is something like: What has been capturing my attention? They may find that gender issues have been foremost in their minds, or they might realize that they have tended to write about the struggles of the poor. Perhaps they have focused often on the ways they and their friends are isolated from each other in school, or maybe they are concerned about the possibility of a war breaking out in some region of the world. Environmental concerns, looks-ism in the media, or care for the elderly may have come up, even tangentially, in several entries, taking on new importance as they take shape in the writer's mind on this rereading. Some students may realize, upon rereading their recent entries, that they have never written about the issues they care most about, and so they might need to turn their attention in a new direction now, making several entries about something that matters to them. By surveying the journey of thought they have made recently, writers allow a topic to choose them; confronted

with the evidence of their own attentive noticing, they may realize for the
first time that there are political concerns they care about.

Perhaps it is obvious that writers' rereading of their notebooks should not
be limited to the entries they have made since the class formally began
turning its attention to social critique. Because political issues—imbalances,
silences, associations—are everywhere, constantly present in everyone's life,
even earlier notebook entries that at first seemed like "personal" stories or
thoughts also contain possibly critical material. To spot the political potential
in personal writing, students need to reread these entries employing lenses
similar to those they've been applying to the world:

- Embedded within some entries might be issues of *fairness and setting
  things straight*. Very often, the impulse to write was the complaint that
  some adult action was unfair, but in the margins or in a new entry, students can develop their ideas about how things can be made more fair.

- Some entries lend themselves to *trying on the perspectives of others*.
  Perhaps the student has already begun, writing, "maybe she thought that
  . . . ." If not, the student can look for opportunities to consider an event
  or situation from multiple points of view. This is helpful because, in many
  ways, it is the essence of imagining toward social action.

- Some entries may be able to lead the writer to think about questions of
  what people need for happiness and well-being. What is it that makes
  it possible to have a good life? Does everybody need the same things?
  Who has those things and who does not? How could it be possible for
  more people to participate in a happy, well-lived life?

- It is more frequently possible than one would think to find opportunities to *follow the money* in student writing. After all, many of the events
  that excite them or upset them have economic underpinnings. Focusing thinking on money itself, where it comes from and where it goes,
  can lead toward important socially critical perspectives.

- Naturally, a critical habit of mind involves *questioning authority*. Fortunately for our purposes, it is also an adolescent habit of mind, and so
  we can help students to use their rebellious impulses productively in
  their political thinking. They may ask themselves: Why is this so? Who
  benefits from this? Who says it has to be this way?

- *Feelings of anger and indignation* often contain implicit critique beneath
  them. It is sometimes difficult, but always important, to help students
  differentiate the anger that stems from their own sense of entitlement
  from a more righteous indignation in response to unfairness. Feelings of

empathy and compassion are the positive face of social critique and may be just as useful in helping students to imagine themselves doing something to help someone else.

- One could probably read every entry in a writer's notebook as embodying a theme of *identity and affiliation*. Writing that is for-the-writer often wrestles with issues of what sort of person the writer wants to be, or how she wants to view herself. Becoming a particular sort of person involves figuring out which other people I most want to be like. Who we are is partly a function of what team we are on.

- Seeds of social action can be found in any entry that involves getting people together to do something. Thinking about *collective action*, even if it is not especially political in purpose, can help students draw on familiar experiences in order to imagine coming together with others to explore and pursue more complex common social agendas. Entries about baseball teams may provide the vision for ways of gathering people together to improve the quality of the water in the town.

- Personal entries often, implicitly, carry themes of *difference*. The realization that we are not all alike provides many of the axes along which we affiliate, and also brings attention to many social inequalities that need addressing. Socially penetrating differences may occur along the lines of family structure, culture, race, sexuality, class, gender, or age. Naturally, just the noticing of difference, or even an extended analysis of difference, does not dictate what is to be done about it.

From Listening to the World to Talking Back

I have focused in this article on the thinking that might lead to social action, but I hope it is clear that this work in a writer's notebook, to be complete, has to lead to writing for readers. Students need to follow through on their initial thoughts with the inquiry process and the writing process, individually and collaboratively. In so doing, they say to readers in the real world: "Look at this! I've been noticing and questioning this thing that is happening in the world. I want you to notice it and question it, too. And I want us to work together to make it better." Writing for social action is thus a conversation with the world, involving both listening and answering, about how we all live together in the world.

We want students to be able to continue their dialogues with the world beyond the time that we know them, carrying what they learn in our classroom community out into the other communities through which they move in their lives. In order to do so, they need to know how to identify problems and possibilities, to think about given realities while envisioning better potential worlds. Maxine Greene has called for "teaching to the end of arousing a consciousness of membership, active and participant membership in a society of unfulfilled promises—teaching for . . . a wide-awakeness that might make injustice unendurable" (1998, p. xxx). This consciousness, this wide-awakeness can be born in students' writing in notebooks, if they use the work in the notebook as a lens with which to examine their world. It is time for us as teachers to invite students to wake up to their world in their writing to think.

References

Bomer, R. (1995). *Time for meaning: Crafting literate lives in middle and high school*. Portsmouth, NH: Heinemann.

Bomer, R. (1998). Transactional heat and light: More explicit literacy learning. *Language Arts, 76*, 11–18.

Freire, P. (1992). *Pedagogy of hope: Reliving pedagogy of the oppressed*. (R. R. Barnes, Trans.). New York: Continuum.

Freire, P., & Macedo, D. (1987). *Literacy: Reading the word and the world*. South Hadley, MA: Bergin & Garvey.

Greene, M. (1998). *Teaching for social justice*. In W. Ayers, J. A. Hunt, and T. Quinn (Eds.), Teaching for social justice (pp. xxvi–xlvi). New York: Teachers College Press.

Tharp, R., & Gallimore, R. (1988). *Rousing minds to life: Teaching, learning, and schooling in social context*. Cambridge, UK: Cambridge University Press.

III AESTHETIC APPRECIATION VERSUS CRITICAL INTERROGATION

Aesthetic appreciation and critical interrogation are often emphasized to the exclusion of one or the other. Good teaching allows for artistic expression and appreciation, but it also always pushes intellectual and social processing. Elizabeth Radin Simons, Kathy Daniels, Junia Yearwood, and Darcelle Walker's "Diversifying Curriculum in Multicultural Classrooms" demonstrates a synthesis of these two important goals in their classroom instruction and curriculum planning. In "Where Art and Life Intersect," Carol Jago continues this necessary instructional dialectic by providing insightful biographical and historical information to accompany instructional suggestions for teaching Nikki Giovanni's poetry. Randi Dickson extends this notion still further by having her students compose poetic reflections of their visits to nursing homes.

Taking a different path, Albert B. Somers asks, " How much about the teaching and learning of poetry should we try to evaluate and what forms should the evaluation take?" In his essay assessing poetry instruction, he explores traditional and authentic assessment of poetry teaching and learning. Anthony J. Scimone completes the section by reflecting on student-centered poetry instruction.

11 Diversifying Curriculum in Multicultural Classrooms: "You Can't Be What You Can't See"

Elizabeth Radin Simons, with Kathy Daniels,
Junia Yearwood, and Darcelle Walker

The M-CLASS teachers agreed that the curriculum should include authors who reflected the faces in their classrooms. They also wanted it to address the questions about race and ethnicity that were on their minds and on those of their students. In this chapter, diversifying or broadening the curriculum refers to expanding the literature, making it more multicultural and refocusing classroom goals to address issues of race and ethnicity.

Although M-CLASS teachers agreed on the need for diversification of curriculum, they differed in their reasons. Many teachers of color spoke with a special urgency about broadening the curriculum. Roberta Logan, who was both a teacher and one of the site coordinators in Boston, and who is African American, explained:

> You can look at something from many points of view and sort of dismiss multiculturalism. But I'm not in that position. I'm not in the position to do that because I'm always looking with a double lens. The lens of the outsider, the lens of the person of color. So that when I look [for example] at a textbook, I say, "What topics are we covering and how are we covering them?" I'm always keenly aware. (Local meeting, Boston, January 7, 1993)

Originally published as Chapter 8 of *Inside City Schools,* edited by Sarah Warshauer Freedman et al., a co-publication of NCTE and Teachers College Press. Copyright 1999 Teachers College, Columbia University.

At the same meeting Junia Yearwood, who is also African American, wondered how people could question diversification of the curriculum. Yearwood considers diversification critical not only for her students but for the survival of American democracy.

> [It] validates your existence. [It says,] "I'm important too. Look at me, I'm here!" To me it seems simple. To the academic world, it's a big issue. They're talking about how it factionalizes, it brings down cohesiveness. But what good is cohesiveness if it's built on lies, if it's built on exclusion of other people. I don't see how inclusion could weaken society. (Local meeting, Boston, January 7, 1993)

At another meeting later in the year, Yearwood talked of the dangers of a mainstream America that is ignorant of minorities. Changing the curriculum is about "survival," Yearwood said, ". . . because this society is structured [with] the dominant group teaching and ignorant of what the minority group is fussing about all the time, [so] you have problems!" Darcelle Walker, another African American, agreed with Yearwood and added, "You have a minority group who's not learning about themselves either!" (site meeting, Boston, May 23, 1993). These teachers see two benefits of broadening the curriculum: "The dominant group" will learn about people other than themselves, and people of color will see themselves represented and studied in the classroom.

Susanna Merrimee, a Chinese American teacher in San Francisco, interpreted the tension over curriculum, to which Yearwood was referring, as a struggle for power. "When I come across the word [*multiculturalism* in the curriculum]," she wrote, "I see different kinds of ethnic groups struggling for power. I see tension. I see the winners, and I see those who are defeated. How do we ensure the silent ones can have a voice?" (site meeting, San Francisco, June 12, 1993). African American teachers in separate cities, James Williams and Brenda Landau McFarland, like Merrimee, focused on sharing power. Williams wrote that multiculturalism in the curriculum was "the willingness of people of different cultures to share with others who are different" (site meeting, Boston, October 31, 1992). Landau McFarland added that it is "the actual ability to accept other cultures without feeling threatened" (site meeting, Chicago, October 18, 1992).

School curriculum is often prescribed by the state and the city and reflects the political power structure. The teachers of color just quoted here look at America through the lens of a person of color. They have experienced racism and argue for a multicultural curriculum, to validate racial and ethnic groups and, at the same time, to educate American students about racial and ethnic groups. In this way, it is hoped, students will learn not to be threatened by difference and to share political power.

It is important to stress that the White teachers do not disagree with these points made by teachers of color. But White teachers, as well as some teachers of color, in their arguments for a diversified curriculum, emphasized the richness found in diversity, the importance of honoring diversity, and the commonalties we share across ethnic groups. Kathy Daniels, a White teacher in Chicago, wrote that multicultural education "means recognizing and celebrating the diversity in the country. Recognizing and celebrating the richness that can come from that diversity. And finally recognizing and celebrating those things that we have in common" (site meeting, Chicago, October 18, 1992). Nancy O'Malley, a White teacher from Boston said, "It's a real respect for the equality and the individuality" of the students (site meeting, Boston, May 23, 1993). Verda Delp, a White teacher from San Francisco, described multicultural curriculum "as honoring individual cultural diversity" (site meeting, San Francisco, October 22, 1992).

These reasons for using multicultural curriculum did not preclude political issues. Delp continued, "I do believe that teachers need to empower kids and give them the skills of literacy, and in order to do that you have to give them the powers that make them succeed in the White world. But does that assume that therefore I think that's the power structure that should be, is that a racist thing?" (site meeting, San Francisco, October 22, 1992). Delp's question led to discussion about the importance of teaching literacy skills, what it means to question the power structure, and what it means to assimilate.

In "The Silenced Dialogue: Power and Pedagogy in Educating Other People's Children," one of the first articles the M-CLASS teachers read, Lisa Delpit (1988) writes about the "different lenses" of White and Black teachers. She recommends:

> We must learn to be vulnerable enough to allow our world to turn upside down in order to allow the realities of others to edge them-selves into our consciousness. In other words, we must become ethnographers in the true sense. (p. 297)

In teacher-research projects such as M-CLASS, inner-city teachers of color and White inner-city teachers can come together as "ethnographers," open up to each other's realities and further the dialogue on multicultural education.

The M-CLASS ethnographers found that two types of models were fundamental to their students' success. The first was the teachers themselves; the second was found in the portraits in multicultural texts of people like and unlike themselves. Through both of these models, students can stretch their cultural knowledge and find both heroes and warning tales. At a meeting in Chicago, Stephanie Davenport quoted her minister, who in talking about the dilemma of many young people today, said, "You can't be what you can't see." Students need models of what they can be.

No matter what their argument for diversifying curriculum, teachers agreed on two ideas that underlie a successfully diversified curriculum. First, it must be ethnically and racially inclusive and explicitly address issues of race, ethnicity, and prejudice. Second, in order to successfully deliver this curriculum, teachers must have empathy and concern for the students for whom they will be acting as models and guiding through some volatile issues. This second theme was labeled "caring" at the last Boston site meeting when the teachers were reviewing the 24 papers written by members of the M-CLASS project. Roberta Logan observed:

> There's an ethos of caring throughout the papers, you . . . care for your subject [and] . . . you care for children, and they blend together, but there's a definite ethos of caring and responsibility. (Site meeting, Boston, May 23, 1993)

The "ethos of caring" as defined by Logan encompasses students and subject matter. Caring takes multiple forms, beginning with the more obvious, to like and enjoy the students and to believe in their potential. Less obvious forms of caring are revealed in the responsibilities implicit in caring (some of these overlap the first theme): the responsibility to design a multicultural curriculum in which students can see reflections of themselves and models of whom they might become; to create curriculum through which they can engage reluctant students; to risk addressing the volatile questions; and to teach the necessary literacy skills.

This chapter presents the work of three teachers, Kathy Daniels, of Chicago, and Junia Yearwood and Darcelle Walker, both from Boston, whose research addressed the broadening of curriculum. The complex variables surrounding the two themes of diversification and caring are demonstrated through the research of three inner-city teachers teaching different multiethnic populations in different settings. Daniels works with students who are unskilled and disengaged; Yearwood's case study student is skilled but disengaged; and Walker's students are both skilled and engaged.

Daniels's challenge is to interest her students in school and develop their reading and writing skills. Yearwood focuses on students' self-image and how reading can influence self-image and have an impact on learning. She has a theory about how to motivate students based on her adolescent experience of self-discovery through reading about other Blacks such as herself. Walker's research question, like Yearwood's, comes from an adolescent experience of extreme ethnic discomfort over a text read in class. Walker investigates students' comfort level reading literature depicting racism.

Developing Interest in Reading: Kathy Daniels

Faced with the challenge of teaching high school freshmen 3 to 4 years below grade level, Kathy Daniels set about changing her curriculum, pedagogy, and class size. The previous year, with a colleague, she had proposed a restructuring effort at her school, using both ESEA (Elementary and Secondary Education Act) and Chapter I funds, to create small classes for low-skilled students. Their proposal was adopted by the Chicago Board of Education as an "innovative organizational approach," and they were able to create two classes of 10 students and order a new set of teenage fiction with multicultural themes. It was in one of these classrooms that Daniels did her research. The introduction from her M-CLASS research report establishes the context for her work.

> I have been teaching English at Farragut High School for more than 16 years, and three things have remained pretty constant during that time. First, the reading scores of 75% of our entering freshmen are below grade level. Second, gangs and racial tension have been serious issues in the community. Only the complexion of the school has changed. When I arrived, 85% of the students were African American, and 15% were Latino. Today, the school is almost 90% Latino (mostly Mexican) and a little more than 10% African American. Gangs are formed along racial lines and gang activity has escalated in the past 4 or 5 years. When a fight breaks out in school, even if it begins with two individuals, it quickly explodes out of control. When something gang related happens in the community we can expect to see its effects—either continuation or retaliation—in school the next day.
>
> The third constant is that the great majority of our students have always been good kids who respond to kindness, sensitivity, and respect—kids who want to do better, who want a life without violence, who still have some hope for the future, and who are willing to keep trying. It is for them that I keep trying too.
>
> Against the backdrop of violence, I'm still looking for answers. What do we do about kids who come to high school reading 3 or 4 years below level? Actually, in all my years at Farragut, I have only known a handful of students who truly *couldn't* read, in other words, decode,

but too many of them didn't read and didn't care about reading. . . .
I have had a "gut feeling" that the only approach that would work was
one that was centered in real reading and writing. This belief was based
partly on my experiences with journals at another school in the late
1960s. . . . When I rather timidly suggested this idea, some of my colleagues at Farragut reminded me that my previous school was all
White and middle class, and they assured me that it wouldn't work
with "our kids" because "our kids" just couldn't read!

Despite the almost desperate conditions of this environment, Daniels
recognized that the students wanted to learn. Moreover, for 16 years she had
been observing these students and saw what her colleagues overlooked—
that despite low test scores, the students arrived with reading and writing
skills that she could build on. Daniels hypothesized that her students would
be better served by a structured workshop approach to reading than by the
decontextualized skills pedagogy advocated by some of her colleagues.

Daniels, who radiates warmth and humor, is a magnet for students. They
flock to her with questions about both school and life as she walks down the
corridors and when she sits at her desk in the teachers' lounge. Her
classroom is decorated with photos she takes of each student in the first
weeks of school. These accompany write-ups of interviews her students have
done of each other. She begins the year asking the students to tell her about
the high and low points of their lives. She gets to know them from the start,
and they get to know her. As Delpit (1988) suggests, she offers the students
her world, taking the risk of sharing personal stories, even silly ones, to edge
her life into their reality.

I try to set the tone of community in our classroom the first day by
telling them about myself—my life at Farragut and my life outside of
school—and then inviting them to tell me about themselves and their
reactions to Farragut in their first journal entry. I told them about my
cat Fluffy and how goony she was. I told them that I had two children.
. . . I also told them that I don't have many rules in my classroom, but
the major one is that we respect each other and work together to help
one another, that no matter what goes on outside, it doesn't come into
the class.

I hoped that they would recognize my respect for them and feel
safe enough to be honest even in those early entries, and they were.
The first journal entries showed the concerns one might expect from
freshmen, as well as some others. Elena wrote about the difficulty of
finding the classrooms, but she also said, "I wish I could get a education because right now I'm nobody just a freshman. Wen I graduate from H.S Im going to be somebody because for now Im nobody."
I responded, "Even freshmen are somebody!" Later in the same entry,

> I assured her that it would get better. Melissa wrote that she thought she would be scared and get lost, but she added, "This is my second day here at Farragut and I almost know how to be in the halls and how to go to my classes." Eduardo told about his family and his interest in football, but also wrote, "Most of my friends were dropouts. But I am going to stay in school." My response was, "I hope you *do* stay in school!"

Even in their first journals, Daniels's students were candid, offering her their reality. She wrote back assuaging their fears, such as Elena's concern that she was "nobody." Daniels encouraged them academically, not didactically telling them what to do, but expressing her personal hope for them, as when she wrote to Eduardo, "I hope you *do* stay in school."

The journal writing, one piece of Daniels's writing curriculum, served multiple purposes: Students were learning how to communicate through writing and they were getting personal attention from Daniels. At the same time, Daniels was laying the groundwork for the reading workshop, where students would also keep a journal. The early journals were informal and unstructured. Their reading-workshop journals, although retaining the informality, would be built around specific questions designed to teach skills of summary and analysis. Now, in the beginning of the year, caring and curriculum intertwined; teacher and students were getting to know one another through their informal correspondence while students practiced their writing and reading skills.

In the first few months of the school year Daniels talked with her teacher-research group about incidents in her class, incidents that demonstrate her continual care in building community for her students and that show how she was slowly and deliberately connecting the students to school and thus to learning. In mid-October several students were considering transferring to another school and were discussing the move *sotto voce* during class. Because of the small class size, Daniels overheard the conversation and told the class, "Well y'know if any one of you transfer, it will really affect all of us. I mean that would really be *sad*." The students were jolted and said, "You mean you really would mind, you mean you really would miss us?" and made her repeat her statement. As Daniels observed, "That's kind of neat so early in the year, and it wouldn't happen in a bigger class" (site meeting, Chicago, October 18, 1992).

Also in October, Daniels mentioned to a Mexican American boy that her family liked a salad she made with *nopales*. The incredulous student blurted out, "You like Mexican food?" Daniels had risked the corniest of connections, the one often dismissed as patronizing and as avoiding the hard issues; she shared her love of a part of the culture of her students. Daniels explains, "That's a kind of a recognition for them. Here's this Anglo teacher and she knows some of this. So, I think that's a real teeny teeny part of it" (site meeting, Chicago, October 18, 1992). Sharing a love of food is not false deference or condescension as long as it is part of a larger picture of concern, teaching strategies, and expanded curriculum.

Daniels had planned to start the reading workshop in the fall. By February, impatient with district snafus that delayed the arrival of the multicultural books she had ordered, she made do with what she could buy and find at school, teenage fiction written by White authors. By now Daniels and her students knew each other well. The students did not yet find pleasure in reading, but they trusted her promise that together they would find books they would want to read. To set up her reading workshop, over and over again Daniels modeled through her enjoyment of reading the importance of the activity. She also stressed finding books of genuine interest to each student. To foster individual taste in reading, Daniels told her students to reject any book they didn't like. "This particular aspect of choice must be a new one for them," she wrote, "they all tested it out frequently!" Daniels's description of the first weeks of readers' workshop reveals the patience, effort, and time she put into finding the exact book to match each student's interest.

> Two of the girls, Tuana and Sandra, had a difficult time finding a book that they liked well enough to read all the way through. They started several, read 20 or 30 pages, and then switched to something else. Finally, I found an old set of books in the English book room titled *Gang Girl*. Both girls finally settled down. Tuana finished the book in a week and wrote in her response journal, "This book is about a girl that was 14 and she had a friend that was in a gang and she felt lonly and she joined in and she never thout she was going to be the leader. She had an exsedent and she regret what she had done. Its a great book its like real life and I would like to read another book like that."
>
> The next day, after I read Tuana's journal, I questioned her about what she meant by "real life." She decided that she meant that she could identify with the main character, who was a girl faced with many of the same problems that she and her friends had to face, such as the decision to join a gang. Now my job was to find "another book like that."
>
> When Juan was reading *Durango Street*, he wrote, "Im reading a book called Durango street. Each day I read it, it gets better and better. I'm going to read this book untill I finish reading it." Eduardo chose a book called *The Perfect Crime* and wrote in his response jour-

nal, "The book is getting pretty exciting and I met keep the book after all." The day that Melissa finished reading *The Divorce Express* by Paula Danziger, she wrote, "I just finished reading 'The Divorce Express.' It's a nice book about two parents of two girls who are divorced and they become good friends. Rosies mom and Phoebes father are going out so now they are like sisters. I recomend it to girls."

After several false starts, I offered Manuel (who told me he hates to read) a book called *Chico*, mostly because it's short and easy. It turns out that the teenage hero has some of the same problems Manuel himself faced, and he eagerly picked up the book each time we had a reading-workshop period and read with a concentration and intensity that he had not shown previously. He moved to the back of the room where no one would disturb him. The other students were aware of what was happening.

Daniels's students connected to these books in multiple ways. Often the link was situational, as in *Gang Girl* and *Divorce Express*. But Daniels noticed another interesting connection: students read ethnicity into texts that were not ethnic but that depicted their lives; this happened with *Gang Girl*. Sometimes the connection was ethnic, as in Manuel's reading of *Chico*. In fact, Daniels thought Manuel connected to this book on several levels, since both Chico and Manuel had alcoholic fathers.

The daily response journals show the value of Daniels's experiment with the reading workshop with her underskilled, disengaged freshmen. The students were beginning to enjoy reading. Tuana liked her book about "real life" so much that she was willing to try another. Juan was learning that a book can hook him and get better and better. Melissa was recommending a book. Manuel liked reading for the first time because he saw himself on the page. Students were learning some basic literacy skills as they summarized and gave broad critiques of books. They were learning to select books of interest, rejecting ones they did not like after 20 or so pages, and they were recommending books to one another.

Research from the educational establishment that questions the importance of smaller class size in learning goes against the grain for teachers. Daniels's study offers some useful insights into why class size can make a difference, especially for students who do not trust school, and for teachers and students of different ethnicities trying to make personal connections. They need time to get to know and trust one another, which is easier in a small class. In a small class Daniels could more readily personalize the curriculum, have one-on-one talks and regular writing exchanges with each student. She could respond immediately to the reading

journals, as she did with Tuana, and have the time to find "another book like
that." Because the class was a small supportive community, there could be,
early into the reading workshop, a moment like the class response when
Juan called out, "Manuel finished *Chico!*" and everyone cheered. In a small
class, Daniels could tell a student he would be missed—in a large class, in
October a student might barely be known, let alone missed. Moreover,
because of the quick buildup of trust, students could accept as sincere
Daniels's concern about the loss of one of them and what it would mean to
the group.

Out-of-school bragging about a class in inner-city schools is extremely
rare. Daniels's students grew proud of the class and told their friends, who
began to appear in class. Daniels wrote, "Kids who had study or lunch or
whose teacher was absent that day, sometimes they came in and did their
homework. Sometimes they selected a book and read along with us."

Daniels's students experienced the creation of a strong classroom
community by a caring teacher. In the small class, reading young adult
fiction, they made a 180-degree turn in their attitude toward school and
began to enjoy reading. Daniels regretted that she would not be their teacher
the following year. In this first year she had succeeded in getting them
reading, even enjoying it. A 2nd year could have solidified their change,
improved their reading and writing skills, and allowed time for more
challenging literature.

Knowing One's History and School Success: Junta Yearwood

Departures from the status quo in school—departures necessary for
capturing the attention of disinterested, inner-city students—require
structural changes in the school. Such changes are enormously time
consuming and difficult to accomplish, especially for teachers who often
don't have the leverage to make change. Yet just as Daniels created a
new small class, Yearwood, in an attempt to turn around failing students,
made two changes: She created a multicultural library for her school and
designed a new freshmen course called Personal Growth. Yearwood, an
English teacher, agreed to develop and teach Personal Growth, a one-
semester social-living course, in order to address what she saw as a
major cause of her students' failure, their lack of knowledge of the
history of their race or ethnicity and a lack of positive ethnic role models.
Yearwood's belief is rooted in a life-changing moment in her
adolescence:

> As a Black woman of African and West Indian descent . . . upon
> learning my history, I acquired a strong sense of who I was and devel-
> oped a sense of pride, importance, and purpose. This occurred . . .
> in my early teens [in Barbados], when I first learned about the his-
> tory of my African ancestors in class, the horrors of slavery, and the
> strength and resilience of my people. . . . I became extremely moti-
> vated to find out as much as I could about my heritage.

The history curriculum in Yearwood's own school in Barbados did not
include West Indian history, only that of Britain and Europe. As an
adolescent, on her own she went to the library and learned about the
"strength and resilience of [her] people." After emigrating to Boston, she
continued to read widely in ethnic literature, which reinforced her
convictions about the value of knowing one's roots, Reading Malcolm X's
sentence, "Just as a tree without roots is dead, *a people without history or
cultural roots also becomes a dead people* [emphasis added]" (p. 25),
Yearwood reflected on its meaning for her students:

> "Dead" students have no desire to learn. Dead students do not under-
> stand the importance of learning. Dead students cannot learn from
> the mistakes of the past. Dead students have no sense of their his-
> tory and, therefore, do not value the present, and have no goals for
> the future! To educators, dead students are a liability; dead students
> are not successful and thereby prove us to be failures.

Yearwood offered a remedy for "dead" students:

> When you see yourself in a history book, when your people are
> referred to in the history book doing . . . positive things, then it does
> something to your desire to learn. It does something to your self-
> worth, to your pride, to your self-esteem. (Local meeting, Boston, Jan-
> uary 7, 1993)

In her research, Yearwood wanted to see if the epiphany she had
experienced in discovering her history in Barbados was relevant to her
students in Boston in the 1990s.

Anyone walking into Yearwood's classroom of African American, Latino,
White, Asian, Middle Eastern, Cape Verdean, African, and West Indian
students knows immediately that she cares about these students. English
High School in Boston, where she teaches, looks and feels like a locked-
down prison. But when the door opens to Yearwood's room, one sees
sunlight coming through high-set windows that run the length of the far wall.
Below these a shelf overflows with flourishing plants. The other three walls
are covered with inspirational sayings mounted on colored paper, looking
like fields of multicolored flowers. Many students, however, do not arrive

eager to learn, so Yearwood tries different curricular approaches to catch their attention. Before she can teach them literacy skills, they need to have a stake in school. The ultimate goal of her Personal Growth course, which includes her multicultural library, is to help students learn the value of education. At the San Francisco conference that began the M-CLASS project, Yearwood listened to a discussion about teen culture. Realizing its pivotal role in her students' self-image and attitude toward school, she added it to Personal Growth. Her students' reflections on their teen culture produced some disturbing writing. One journal read:

> Teens feel that school isn't that important in our life. . . . We don't understand why we need to learn so many different things. The youth culture make[s] me not want to learn. That's the effect it has. In school you have to watch your back . . . sometimes you don't even want to come to school, other teens make fun of you. (Site meeting, Boston, October 31, 1992)

Yearwood envisioned her Personal Growth class as an opportunity to combat the negative power of youth culture and the racial and ethnic self-deprecation she saw in many of her students. Personal Growth directly addressed the aspects of her students' lives that Yearwood believed severely interfered with school, such as lack of self-esteem, confusion about self-identity, puberty, peer pressure, friendship, drugs, gangs, violence, anger, racism, and prejudice. While studying these topics, students would learn critical thinking skills in decision making, goal setting, and career choices. Since self-esteem and self-image are linchpins of academic success, Yearwood opened with a 2-week introductory unit on identity where she introduced race and ethnicity, themes maintained throughout the semester.

During this first unit, Yearwood introduced the students to the multicultural library, which she physically brought into the room, on a large rolling cart. The library, the informational backbone of Personal Growth, was also a vehicle for teaching literacy skills. The library contained biography and autobiography by writers from many races and ethnicities, professions and walks of life, the famous and the ordinary. Yearwood had contributed many of her own books to the library, which covered a wide range of reading levels and interests. It included works by Toni Morrison and Alice Walker as well as recent popular books about athletes, television personalities, and movie stars. Like Daniels, Yearwood attempted to catch the interest of all her students.

In Yearwood's experience, her male students were less likely to be readers. Therefore on the day that she dramatically rolled in her library cart, she kept her eye on the males. She instructed the students to browse and choose a book. "All of my male students eagerly chose a book," Yearwood wrote, "and there was utter silence for the next 35 minutes as they read. With rare exceptions, students chose books that reflected their ethnicity and culture." Most, she noticed, chose the books by their covers, scanning them for faces like their own. Throughout the semester, while studying the Personal Growth topics in class, students continued to read independently from Yearwood's library.

For her research, Yearwood followed one student, Robert, and his use of the multicultural library. Robert was born in Cape Verde of Portuguese and African parents and came to the United States at the age of 4. He self-identified as Black. Yearwood interviewed Robert throughout the semester and continued to do so for several years after. Early on, he told her, "I always saw White people as being heroes and Blacks as inferior, low-life druggies." Yearwood was not surprised; she has seen vestiges of this attitude in her own family:

> This quote from my student, Robert, reinforces what I've known for most of my life: . . . the lack of knowledge of one's heritage contributes to one's lack of positive self-esteem, which in turn fosters self-hatred. . . . Robert's perceptions of Whites and Blacks are no different from thxose of my acquaintances, friends, family members, and even my own mother, from whom I've heard similar statements of self-deprecation.

In class, Robert was a leader, and others listened to him, but he was the kind of leader who orchestrated trouble and got suspended. His junior high school cumulative record was a roller coaster of semesters with straight Fs followed by semesters of As and Bs. He was capable, alternately attentive and disruptive. While taking Personal Growth, his grades went up in most subjects. His English teacher reported improvement in his writing, which Robert attributed to the extensive reading he was doing in Personal Growth.

Yearwood was interested in monitoring Robert's attitude toward Blacks. He told her that he knew where he had learned that Blacks were inferior; it's "because of what I saw on TV and what I was taught in elementary school . . . that Whites were better than Blacks." Yearwood then asked him, "Did your elementary teachers actually say this?" Robert explained:

> No, but the only thing they ever taught me was about slavery. They never explained why Blacks became slaves. Nothing else, just the fact that Blacks were slaves. I had a very negative opinion of Blacks.

Robert's school experience in the United States wasn't much different from Yearwood's in Barbados. In Personal Growth, Robert became a voracious reader. He preferred biographies of famous African Americans—Malcolm X, Dick Gregory, and Dr. Martin Luther King, Jr. Reading these books, he realized, perhaps for the first time, that in America there were Black heroes. He began to notice African American heroes in popular culture; viewing television with a new perspective, he saw Arsenio Hall, Montel Williams, Oprah, and Bill Cosby as role models. After a semester of immersing himself in Yearwood's multicultural library, Robert saw some practical value in what he was reading. He told Yearwood, "Students of all races should learn their culture in American schools so that they wouldn't feel inferior to Americans, and they should learn it and be proud so they wouldn't get put down."

One way to measure Robert's change in racial identity is with Tatum's (1992) model of racial identity development for Blacks. In the first stage, Tatum posits that Blacks internalize the idea that "White is right." Robert began there. During the semester he moved toward a later stage where he had a more secure sense of his own racial identity. As he told Yearwood, the information he learned made him proud and gave him the knowledge to defend himself against "put-downs." Furthermore, he was able to get beyond self-interest to suggest that all students could benefit from similar experiences.

Like most M-CLASS teachers, Yearwood describes herself as strict—no hats in class, no bad language, only respectful behavior. At the end of the semester Robert reported some changes in his own behavior to Yearwood, "I don't call people names and stuff. . . . I don't call females 'bitches' and I'm not rude. . . . I also try to teach my friends things because some of my friends are real ignorant." It's probably not far-fetched to say that Robert, seeing a caring teacher modeled in Yearwood, has in a small way taken the teacher role on himself.

At the end of the year, with a laugh, Yearwood admitted to her teacher-research group that Robert's response to Personal Growth and the multicultural library was something of a best-case scenario. He read voraciously, even right through the night on occasion. Not all students became avid readers, but the great majority evaluated the unit with thanks to Yearwood for giving them the opportunity to learn about themselves and to be proud of their heritage.

Yearwood and Personal Growth, however, did not immediately change the course of Robert's life. The following year, he was dismissed from the school. Along with others, Yearwood helped to find him a good alternative school where he could study drama, a field he liked; but he dropped out. Lost for a while, he kept in touch with Yearwood, visiting her at school, borrowing and returning books from her library. When last heard from, he had completed his GED and was hopeful about starting junior college.

Students sitting in Yearwood's class have an inspirational model. They see an African Caribbean woman who believes that her students want to learn—even when they arrive saying that they don't—and who has a well-developed idea about how to help them. They see a teacher who acts on her beliefs, designing and teaching a new course in an effort to turn her students around academically. They see a teacher who furnishes the school with ethnic literature that it had lacked and that she deems critical for her students. She includes books from her own library, an intimate, personal offering to the students through which she models liking books enough to buy them, and that shows that she is a reader and that she reads literature of interest to them. Presenting the students with a library of choices, she honors their individual ethnicity and interests. For her students, Yearwood is a living embodiment of the intimate connection of caring and curriculum. Through her actions, her teaching, and the literature, she models what they "can be."

Ethnic Literature and the Comfort Level of Students: Darcelle Walker

Darcelle Walker, like Daniels and Yearwood, is committed to multicultural literature as an important way of helping students "learn about themselves." Whereas Daniels focused on helping students to become readers and Yearwood on building self-esteem through literature, Walker, whose students are more engaged and skilled, takes on a thorny aspect of multicultural literature: the comfort/discomfort level for students when race and ethnicity are depicted in ways that students experience as insulting or painful.

Walker's interest in the comfort level of literature originated in her adolescence. Early in the year she read her written description of the memory to her fellow teacher-researchers at a Boston meeting.

> Several years ago I paused from my teaching, and I noticed one lone Asian face that looked more pathetic and more uncomfortable than any face I had ever seen before. I realized that this student was inter-nalizing and feeling very vulnerable about a story I was teaching, "Confessions of a Soldier," by Iris Rosofsky. This story is about an American alcoholic who is describing the roots of his addiction to a group of people at an AA [Alcoholics Anonymous] meeting. He admits shooting down three young, unarmed, Vietnamese men. He describes

the hurt, fear, and pain that the Vietnamese men experienced before
he killed all of them. He describes the subsequent guilt he faced after
this incident and how he had never told anyone about it before AA.

As a teacher, I had taught and discussed this story many times
before. . . . But this time the story was different for me, because I
now felt uncomfortable for my Asian American student, who was
obviously very uncomfortable. It dawned on me that this was the first
time I had had an Asian American student in my class.

The only face that had ever been more pathetic, uncomfortable,
and vulnerable than that was my own. That is why I could empathize
with this student so much. When I was in high school, I was a member of a program called ABC, or A Better Chance. This program
recruited talented minority students to send to private schools or to
public high schools with a wealthy student population. Usually the
students were sent too far away for them to live at home, as was the
case for me. During my high school career, I was often the one and
only Black student in an all-White classroom, and whenever the literature had a negative depiction of a Black person, it had a profound
effect on me.

Walker paused and told the group, "This is hard to read," and continued:

> I felt the teachers had no empathy for my comfort level and I also
> developed a hatred for certain types of literature, like *Huckleberry
> Finn*. (Site meeting, Boston, March 27, 1993)

It had been many years since Walker's experience, but the memory was fresh
enough to bring tears to her eyes and to those of her listeners. Walker
explained how she experienced *Huckleberry Finn*:

> All I saw was this clever, wise White boy, Huck Finn, who was so
> much smarter than the Black boy, Jim. Jim had to be taught every-
> thing. And he was often called *nigger* more than his God-given
> name. I noticed that my White classmates and teacher were very
> comfortable with this kind of literature, and it was obvious to me why
> that was. I felt then, and not just in retrospect, that my classmates
> were comfortable discussing and analyzing this literature because
> their own race wasn't being demeaned.

Walker has taught for many years at Boston's McCormack Middle School,
which she describes as the "most academically successful middle school in
the city." The students, who come from low-income sections of Boston, are
African American; White; Puerto Rican; Asian American, mostly Vietnamese;
Cape Verdean; and mixed Indian and African American. From the first day of
school, Walker, like Daniels and Yearwood, worked at creating a socially,
emotionally, and intellectually safe classroom for her students:

> I try to establish a classroom of trust and respect for one anothers' cultures at the very beginning of the year. I do that in many different ways, [for example] I . . . tell bilingual students how jealous I am that they can speak more than one language fluently. I tell them that I studied Spanish for 10 years and still can't speak it as well or as easily as I like. [I do this] after I've overheard students in the classroom complaining about or mocking the Hispanic or Asian American students for speaking their native language.

Walker established trust by sharing her vulnerabilities and by modeling over and over again how she would like students to behave in the class through her personal stories. She is a riveting storyteller and very funny. A lasting impression for the visitor to Walker's classes is that the students never start to pack up before the bell rings—almost unheard of in most high school classrooms.

In her research Walker looked at the comfort levels of her multiethnic students through the reading of two short stories, "Confessions of a Soldier," by Iris Rosofsky, and "The Ethics of Living Jim Crow: An Autobiographical Sketch," by Richard Wright. Walker, who is not fearful of controversy in the classroom, chose the two stories "because they were not subtle in their racism," and because they contained unsettling portraits of three of the ethnic groups in the class.

Setting the intellectual and emotional climate for her study, Walker prepared her students by first sharing her own story about *Huckleberry Finn*. She considered this "the most important discussion I had . . . sharing some of my own classroom experiences with them." Then students talked of similar moments in their lives. Walker risked sharing her adolescent distress with her students. When they, through trust in her, were willing to share similar experiences, Walker had created a prereading activity that set the stage for honest reaction to the curriculum to come.

The first assignment was to read "Confessions of a Soldier" and to fill out a response survey. Walker wrote that she was unprepared for the reaction of her five Asian students:

> The first thing I want to mention is that all five of my Asian American students delayed both reading "Confessions of a Soldier" and answering the survey. I panicked and wondered what I had done wrong in preparing them for this study. I felt I would get my best, most personal responses from them—since this story was about Vietnamese soldiers. Each one of them came to me at different times asking if they could finish other lessons before starting "Confessions." I have to admit that this was a first. Never before had all of them required more time than was given the rest of the class. Eventually,

> though, almost 2 weeks after everyone else had finished, my Asian American students turned in thoughtful, detailed responses. Each response seemed carefully thought out, and I could tell that they discussed certain responses together.

Walker concluded that the Asian American students delayed their reading and writing from fear of the text. However, they dealt with their fears by collaborating, creating a study group and talking through their reactions. They sought comfort in numbers.

Walker's finding seems very useful—the importance of "safety in numbers" when reading literature in which one's own ethnicity or race is mistreated or demeaned. She shared some thoughts with the class at the beginning of the year that might have precipitated the Asian American students' study group. She told her students that:

> most people are more comfortable with their own race. To me, that is a natural feeling. But I also let them know that this doesn't mean that they should feel superior or inferior to any other race and subsequently engage in racist, discriminatory behavior. I tell them to learn to respect, admire, learn, and share with other cultures, but to maintain a sense of pride in their own culture.

In an anonymous-response survey to the readings, students identified themselves by race or ethnicity. Besides asking specific questions on the readings, Walker asked, "If you were not influenced by a teacher, parent, and so on, what ethnic literature would you most prefer to read? Why?" Overwhelmingly, students who identified as White answered that they didn't care what they read. A typical response was "It doesn't matter what literature. All cultures are good, none are more interesting than another." Of the students who identified as Black or African American, almost all said they would choose Black literature, adding such comments as "I would learn more about mine [Black] [*word missing*] because I would like to know what people went through to get the opportunity we have today." The other ethnic groups were split between not caring and wanting to read about their own culture.

Walker showed her concern for her students by stretching them intellectually and making them confront their discomfort when reading texts such as the Rosofsky and Wright short stories. She carefully prepared them for their task. Before reading the short stories, which she knew would cause discomfort among her students, Walker created both a socially and intellectually safe environment. She shared her own vulnerability with her junior high school students, telling them in advance that she was researching the question of comfort level and made them collaborators in her research. By choosing her research topic, she modeled her conviction that ethnic literature is important, even while admitting that it can be disturbing or painful to read when it demeans or presents unbearable historical behavior of one's ethnicity, either intentionally or not. Most important, she modeled, through a personal story, her discomfort when reading about racism in literature. At the end of the year Walker evaluated her teacher research:

> One thing that worked for me was that my students felt validated. They were interested in sharing their intimate feelings because first of all they knew it was helping me in my study, but more important, it wasn't ending up in the trash somewhere.

Summary: "You Can Be What You Can See"

The work of Daniels, Yearwood, and Walker supports the M-CLASS theme that effective multicultural curriculum is based on "an ethos of caring for children and subject matter." In common, the three teachers began the year creating visually attractive and psychologically and socially safe environments for their students. Early on, in moving toward creating that environment, they shared their lives, edging themselves into their students' consciousness, while allowing and encouraging their students' realities into theirs (Delpit 1988). The environments set the stage for the major "caring tool" of a multicultural curriculum. The context, the teacher and her students, determined the questions each teacher asked and the literature they used. Daniels chose easy-to-read young-adult literature of high immediate interest to her students. Yearwood focused on literature emphasizing ethnic models to help the students see "who they could be." Walker, as well as Juarez (Chapter 6), focused on literature to help students face the tough realities of a racist society whereas Alford (Chapter 7) used social studies to achieve the same ends.

12 Where Life and Art Intersect

Carol Jago

When her poetry first emerged from the Black Rights Movement in the late 1960s, Nikki Giovanni became almost at once a celebrated and controversial voice for her times. Born in Knoxville, Tennessee, in 1943 and named Yolande Cornelia Giovanni Jr., she was one of the first black poets to achieve stardom. *Black Feeling, Black Talk*, her first book, is a slim volume of revolutionary poems full of passion, anger, frustration, and love. Giovanni wrote these poems while enrolled in the Master of Fine Arts program at Columbia University. One of the purposes of the program was to publish a book. Giovanni completed *Black Feeling, Black Talk*, published it, and then dropped out of the program, figuring that she had fulfilled the program's requirements. In an interview for *Writer's Digest* (February 1989, 33), Nikki Giovanni describes her Cinderella story:

> To get publicity for *Black Feeling, Black Talk*, I got the idea to have a book party at Birdland because I love jazz. I went to see Harold Logan, who was the manager, and said, "Hi, I'm Nikki Giovanni. I'm a poet, and I have a new book, and I'd love to have a book party at Birdland. I know you're dead on Sundays, so that would be a good day. What do I have to do to have a party here?"
>
> He looked at me like I was crazy, but he finally said, "I'll tell you what. You bring me 125 people and you can have the club. But if you bring me 124 people or any less, you owe me $500."
>
> I said, "Fine," but afterward I thought how would I get $500 if I failed. That was a huge amount of money for me in 1969. Anyway, I make up invitations and sent them out to all sorts of groups and that cost me a couple of hundred dollars to start. Then I contacted

---

Reprinted from *Nikki Giovanni in the Classroom* by Carol Jago.

radio stations and asked if I could go on the air to talk about my book party. I figured the midnight audiences are full of readers, so I did a lot of late night shows. I did everything I could do free to ask people to come to Birdland for my book party. I even asked friends like Morgan Freeman, who was a young actor at the time to read from my book and we'd have a kind of Sunday cabaret.

I ended up with a crowd at Birdland that snaked all the way down the street and turned the corner. Birdland is right in the backyard of *The New York Times*, so some reporters happened to look out the window and wondered what the crowd was all about, and came down to investigate. When they found out everyone was there for a poetry reading, they knew they had a story.

The New York Times took a picture of me, which wound up on the front page of the metro section and, because of the publicity, I sold 10,000 books in the next eight months and attracted the attention of some major publishers.

If this sounds like a Cinderella story, remember I made my own slipper. I'm a Midwesterner. I was raised in Cincinnati, and one of the things I think Midwesterners do very well is work hard. We don't expect magic; we make magic.

Between 1967 and 1970, Giovanni published three books of poetry that achieved wide readership in the black community: *Black Feeling, Black Talk* (1967), *Black Judgment* (1968), *Re: Creation* (1970). These early poems are cultural artifacts of those troubled times. The boldness of her revolutionary proclamations and the accessibility of her poems made these volumes big hits on the poetry charts. Displaying not only an entrepreneurial spirit but also a keen awareness of the Black Aesthetic claim that poetry cannot be divorced from music in the African American tradition, Giovanni made several albums of her poetry read in musical settings, some with religious choirs, others with jazz musicians.

But by the early 1970s, the poetry of the Black Revolution had exhausted its market. At the same time, the subject matter for Nikki Giovanni's poetry began to broaden. In 1972, she produced an electric collection of love poems called *My House* which was followed by *The Women and the Men* in 1974. Both brought her critical acclaim and remain in print as single volumes, remarkable testimony to the enduring attraction of these poems to readers.

One of Giovanni's early poems, "Nikki-Rosa," foreshadows the themes that animate the best of her work both early and late. In it, Giovanni describes specific moments from her own childhood. But the images she recalls are more than biographical details; they are evidence to support her premise that growing up black doesn't always mean growing up in hardship.

Nikki-Rosa

childhood remembrances are always a drag
if you're Black
you always remember things like living in Woodlawn
with no inside toilet
and if you become famous or something
they never talk about how happy you were to have your mother
all to yourself and
how good the water felt when you got your bath
from one of those
big tubs that folk in chicago barbecue in
and somehow when you talk about home
it never gets across how much you
understood their feelings
as the whole family attended meetings about Hollydale
and even though you remember
your biographers never understand
your father's pain as he sells his stock
and another dream goes
And though you're poor it isn't poverty that
concerns you
and though they fought a lot
it isn't your father's drinking that makes any difference
but only that everybody is together and you
and your sister have happy birthdays and very good
Christmasses
and I really hope no white person ever has cause
to write about me
because they never understand
Black love is Black wealth and they'll
probably talk about my hard childhood
and never understand that
all the while I was quite happy

— Nikki Giovanni

Prereading

Before reading "Nikki-Rosa," ask students to describe what they envision
when they say or hear that someone has had a "hard childhood." Create a
cluster on the board of all the features of this condition from your students'
point of view.

Then ask students to think about some of the things they experienced as children that might make someone feel sorry for them but that were actually pleasurable. Students are likely to recall having to share a bed with a sibling where there was plenty of squabbling over space but also many sweet secrets shared. Or a student might remember weekly chores like ironing her father's shirts which, though she would never admit it to her mother, made her feel closer to her dad. Students might offer memories of hand-me-down clothes, errands to the store, or left over dinners. Make a list of these on the board and title them "Childhood Remembrances." Save this list.

Reading

Read "Nikki-Rosa" aloud to students and then ask them to read it again to themselves silently. When you feel certain students have done this, have them read the poem a third time, underlining or highlighting all the words and phrases that describe the various pleasures the speaker in the poem remembers experiencing in her "hard" childhood.

Remind students that while this poem may seem to be obviously autobiographical—the title is reasonably strong evidence—a careful reader always considers the speaker in a poem to be separate from the author.

Discussion

To initiate a discussion of this poem, you might want to ask students the following questions. Encourage the discussion to roam where it will, rather than sticking to this list. Remember, requiring students to answer these questions (especially in complete sentences) could probably make them hate the poem forever.

- Did any of the phrases you marked in "Nikki-Rosa" remind you of your own childhood experiences? How did that make you feel about what you read?

- How would you describe the speaker's attitude toward her child-hood? Why do you think she is worried that a biographer will "never understand"?

- What do you think you "understand" about the circumstances of the speaker's childhood? (Push students to be very specific here in order to help them recreate the world in which these childhood remembrances existed.)
- Why do you think Nikki Giovanni chooses to address the reader directly as "you"? What effect did this have on you as a reader? What assumption does this use of the second person make about Giovanni's expectation of who her readers will be?
- How did you interpret the line "And though you're poor it isn't poverty that / concerns you"? If it wasn't poverty that concerned the speaker, what was it that concerned her? (I think it is *joi de vivre* that has always animated Nikki Giovanni as a child, as an adult, and as a poet; but that is only one reader's response and not necessarily what your students will read into this line.)

Potential Minefields

The line "and I really hope no white person ever has cause / to write about me / because they never understand" might cause some students to feel that Nikki Giovanni is casting them as the "bad guys" in this poem. Encourage students to think about how Nikki Giovanni's experience as a black person might lead her to make this generaliztion about white people. Discourage students from relegating such generalizations to the "bad old days" before the Civil Rights movement. If the issue comes up, it is important to discuss the pervasive presence of racism in our own society and how this shapes our generalizations about who we expect will "understand" us and who we expect never will.

Writing

Here is a suggested sequence of activities:

Gathering material: Bring out the list of childhood remembrances that students compiled as a class and ask them to take out a piece of paper and make a list that is uniquely theirs. Let students know that no one need ever see this list and that they should simply try to record as many occurrences from their childhood that they can remember, both important and seemingly inconsequential.

Talk as prewriting: Put students into pairs and have them take turns imagining that they are biographers conducting an interview with a famous person in order to write a book about this person's life. This particular interview should focus on childhood remembrances. When the first interview is complete, students should reverse roles.

Before they begin, make sure students understand exactly what a biography is. For students with limited experience of the genre, borrow an armload of biographies from the school library and let them browse. They need to see the kind of detail biographers include when writing about a famous person's life. If your students are like mine, biographies of sports figures, rock stars, and celebrities like Selena will get their attention more readily than *The Life of Amelia Earhart*.

Writing to explore an idea: Have students imagine that they are back home following the interview with their biographers. Ask them to write a diary entry for the day describing how they felt about being interviewed and what they hoped their biographer "understood" about the childhood remembrances they had described. Suggest that students make references to Nikki Giovanni's poem "Nikki-Rosa" in their diary entry if it seems appropriate.

An Oral History Project: Now that students have some familiarity with the interview process, brainstorm a list of adults they might like to interview about childhood memories. When everyone has a person in mind, create a list of questions that students could ask. Effective interview questions should invite the person being interviewed to muse on his or her experiences; they should not be yes/no or fill-in-the-blank questions. Given that students will be the ones asking the questions, it is vital that they be written in their own words. I have listed a few to seed students' thinking but urge you to encourage your students to come up with their own.

- What do you remember most about your childhood?
- Why do you think this memory has stayed with you?
- What places come to mind when you think about being a kid?
- What people?

If the technology is available, have students tape the interviews and then play them for one another to identify the most evocative details. These will then become the idea seeds for a poem that demonstrates how life and art intersect.

Formal writing assignment: Ask students to select particularly revealing and interesting details from their interviews and then to tease these words and phrasings into a poem. Their drafts may take the form of a story poem in which the writer describes an event from beginning to end. They may also imitate "Nikki-Rosa" and use a series of moments to create a picture of childhood. When students are satisfied with their drafts, have them turn to partners for help with revision. If possible, suggest that students show this draft to the person they interviewed to see if it is true to what they were told. Encourage students to type their poems and present a polished copy to the adult whose history they have tapped.

Autobiography as Art

Nikki Giovanni's essay "On Being Asked What It's Like to Be Black," first appeared in 1969 in US and was later reprinted in *Gemini: An Extended Autobiographical Statement on My First Twenty-Five Years of Being a Black Poet*. Here Giovanni employs a different genre to explore the themes of "Nikki-Rosa." As this essay—written when she was twenty-five years old—demonstrates, Giovanni was outspoken from the start. It also foreshadows the extraordinary lady she has become.

> I've always known I was colored. When I was a Negro I knew I was colored; now that I'm Black I know which color it is. Any identity crisis I may have had never centered on race. I love those long, involved, big-worded essays on "How I Discovered My Blackness" in twenty-five words more or less which generally appear in some mass magazine—always somehow smelling like Coke or Kellogg's corn flakes—the prize for the best essay being a brass knuckle up your head or behind, if you make any distinction between the two. (24)

The article goes on to describe her family history and the kind of people who Giovanni feels helped to make her who she is.

> Now, Mommy was an intellectual, aristocratic woman, which in her time was not at all fashionable. She read, liked paintings, played tennis and liked to party a great deal. Had she been rich she would have followed the sun—going places, learning things and being just generally unable to hold a job and be useful. But Mommy made just one bad mistake in the scheme of things—she sashayed across the Knoxville College campus, hair swinging down to her behind, most probably carrying a tennis racket, and ran into a shin-head Negro with a pretty suit on. He, being warm and friendly and definitely looking for a city girl to roost with, introduced himself. I have always thought that if his name hadn't been exotic she would never have given him a second thought; but Grandfather, whom my mother was

so much like, had a weakness for Romance languages and here comes this smiling dude with Giovanni for a name. Mommy decided to take him home. (28–29)

In the final paragraph, Giovanni explains:

I was trained intellectually and spiritually to respect myself and the people who respected me. I was emotionally trained to love those who love me. If such a thing can be, I was trained to be in power—that is, to learn and act upon necessary emotions which will grant me more control over my life. Sometimes it's a painful thing to make decisions based on our training, but if we are properly trained we do. I consider this a good. My life is not all it will be. There is a real possibility that I can be the first person in my family to be free. That would make me happy. I'm twenty-five years old. A revolutionary poet. I love. (33)

Turning Students' Own Lives into Art

Though born in Knoxville, Tennessee, Nikki Giovanni's family moved to Cincinnati, Ohio, shortly thereafter. Giovanni returned to her birthplace often and spent most summers and holidays with her grandparents and extended family. As this poem demonstrates so beautifully, wherever she traveled, Knoxville remained her true home.

Knoxville, Tennessee[1]

I always like summer
best
you can eat fresh corn
from daddy's garden
and okra
and greens
and cabbage
and lots of
barbecue
and buttermilk
and homemade ice-cream
at the church picnic
and listen to
gospel music
outside
at the church
homecoming
and go to the mountains with
your grandmother

and go barefooted
and be warm
all the time
not only when you go to bed
and sleep

— Nikki Giovanni

After reading this poem aloud, I ask students what they can tell about the speaker from the things Giovanni has chosen to list as what she likes best. Invariably students identify the speaker as black and from the country. I push them to think about what they can tell from the poem about her attitudes, about what they think might be her priorities in life.

I then invite students to write a poem of their own about something, someplace, or someone they like best. My instructions are intentionally vague though I suggest that they use short lines and imitate the list-like quality of Giovanni's poem. Students soon find that they like this technique very much. With very few words they can produce a page full of poetry. I remind them that in order for their poem to replicate the power of Giovanni's poem, their few words must be exceptionally well-chosen.

As students share their poems with the class, we talk about how it feels to use details from their own lives as raw material for their art. Though at first some think I go too far to equate what they have written with what "real poets" create, the more we look for distinctions between their best work and published poetry, the more their objections subside. Life and art intersect in the classroom as well as on stage or in a published volume. Witness their work:

917 Kings Road

I always liked grandma
best
you can bathe
in her thick love
and borscht
and babka
and blintzes
and lots of
homemade pickles
sultry stews
and super sweets

at the dinner table
and listen to Russian radio
inside
where it is always warm
on the couch
and be lost in papa
as he strums his guitar
plays his voice
sings his memories
of how he always
liked grandma
best
—Edward Brodsky

I have no idea why so many students chose to center their poems on the page, but they did, this one to form a Christmas tree:

LA, California

I

always love

Christmas time best.

You go out with your family

Looking for the perfect tree. Coming home

and decorating it,

and watching it grow even more

beautiful as each decoration is added. Waiting for

the special moment when the lights come on. Fascinated with

all the new colors in

the room: red, green, blue, silver.

Going to sleep at nine so I could wake up to

hide the presents before the family wakes up. Anxious

to know what is

under the tree for me. Thanking God over

and over for giving me another Christmas with the

people

I love.

—Angelin Rahnavardan

I always like winter
best
when it is really cold
and I drink hot chocolate
with creamand sugar
and a little bit of honey

I love when it snows
I go outside and have a snowfight
with my friends
go skiing
It is the only time when hiding under
grandma's brown blanket
with a cup of hot tea
feels good and warm
and sleepy

—Farzad Nikmanesh

I always love writing music
Best
Walking to the corner market
And a melody
Pops into my body
And I race home
Singing out loud
Forgetting about the Bisquick
Running into my room
And putting chords down

Sometimes sitting on my bed
Playing the same thing
Over and over
And over
Squeezing out life from a half dead tune

Jammin in Zack's garage
With the amps at eleven
And we're funky
And we're grooving
And then we take
The groove to
The Roxy
Or the Troubadour
Or an all-girls school dance

And afterwards some people are impressed
And afterwards some people say "that sucked"
And afterwards I am impressed
And afterwards I say "that sucked"

And I get discouraged
And never want to write music again

But I'm always writing music
No matter where I am
Or who I'm with
Even if I'm with Susannah
I always like writing music
best

—Alexi Glickman

Then of course there are the students who take an assignment like this one and run with it in a direction the teacher never imagined:

I always like it when I see a pretty girl
You can look at her body
and smile
and legs
and breasts
And her beautiful hair that just makes
You want to go over and start making love to her.

When I meet a girl
I always put a new piece of gum in my mouth
I tell her what she wants to hear
even if it's not completely
true
I give her a few compliments
so she feels special
And after that
As long as she doesn't think you're ugly
you're in there
if you know what
I mean

—Tony Gallo

There is no doubt in my mind that these 17-year-olds understand how life and art can intersect. Nikki Giovanni's simple celebration of the things that she likes best inspired them to look inside their own lives for poetic possibilities.

The Evolution of the Artist

Toward the end of her militant period, Nikki Giovanni wrote "Revolutionary Dreams." In this poem she explores the development of her thinking in ways that help students see how changing one's mind need not invalidate the authenticity of what has been said and written earlier. In fact, it shows growth.

Revolutionary Dreams

i used to dream militant
dreams of taking
over america to show
these white folks how it should be
done
i used to dream radical dreams
of blowing everyone away with my perceptive powers
of correct analysis
i even used to think i'd be the one
to stop the riot and negotiate the peace
then i awoke and dug
that if i dreamed natural
dreams of being a natural
woman doing what a woman
does when she's natural
i would have a revolution

— Nikki Giovanni

Like much of Giovanni's later poetry, "Revolutionary Dreams" continues to advocate change but views revolution as a personal rather than a collective movement. She has said that "the fight in the world today is the fight to be an individual" (NCTE Annual Convention, November 1998).

Further Resources

- For more information about Nikki Giovanni's place within the tradition of African American literature, see *The Norton Anthology of African American Literature* edited by Henry Louis Gates Jr. and Nellie Y. McKay. The volume was first published in 1997. If your school library doesn't have it yet, they should.

- No formal biography of Nikki Giovanni has yet been published, but if students are interested in learning more about her life, I send them to Giovanni's own collection *Gemini: An Extended Auutobiographical Statement on My First Twenty-Five Years of Being a Black Poet* (1976).

Note

1. Artist Larry Johnson has illustrated "Knoxville, Tennessee," and the collaborative work of poet and painter has been published by Scholastic as a children's picture book (ISBN 0-590-47074-4).

13 Quiet Times: Ninth Graders Teach Poetry Writing in Nursing Homes

Randi Dickson

In 1977, three years after I began teaching English in a junior high school, Kenneth Koch published a book called *I Never Told Anybody*. I remember walking down the main street of the village where I lived and seeing it in the window of the bookstore. I was already familiar with Koch's name, having used his *Wishes, Lies, and Dreams* in class. The jacket cover of *I Never Told Anybody* indicated that the poems came out of Koch's work in a nursing home in New York City, where he structured lessons for residents to write poetry, which they dictated to him and his two adult assistants. The poetry, as in *Wishes, Lies, and Dreams*, was built around themes: favorite colors, memories, the most beautiful thing ever seen, music. Much of the poetry reproduced in the book was evocative of an earlier time, memories recreating the 1920s, 1930s, and 1940s, but it was also evidence of the life of the mind inside a nursing home: how people interacted, or didn't; how they spent their days whiling away their hours. I was moved by the excitement with which the nursing home residents had embraced this opportunity to remember the past, as well as to have a chance to say how they felt and thought now.

Many years later I found myself still playing with the idea behind that book. It had remained vaguely in the back of my mind as something that might find its way into my classroom. In 1990, my second year of teaching a ninth grade honors English class, I asked the students at the beginning of the term to start thinking about their ideas and interests for a project that might go beyond the walls of our classroom and in some way "give back" something to the community in which we lived.

Reprinted from *English Journal*, May 1999.

Among the ideas we brainstormed was the suggestion to work in some capacity with our elder population. I found myself thinking again of Koch's work and wondering, "What if . . . ?" What if, instead of adults like Koch and his assistant Kate Farrell, my ninth graders interacted with the residents of nursing homes to write poetry? I checked *I Never Told Anybody* out of the library and read Koch's introductory essay entitled "Teaching Poetry Writing in a Nursing Home." I took notes on the things he said that intrigued and moved me and that I thought might touch my students as well. Koch says of his work with the residents, "Poetry gave them a new reason for looking at things and for remembering them: to say what they thought and felt" (12). He spoke of "possibilities for poetry—in the lives of old people looked back on, in the time they had now to do that, and to think, with a detachment hardly possible to them before" (4). And he said something that particularly resonated with me, "It is such a pleasure to say things, and such a special kind of pleasure to say them as poetry" (6).

I wrote to Koch, who was on leave that year from his teaching job at Columbia University, and told him how I had been interested in the work he had done in the nursing home. I wondered if he thought it would be possible to have my students work with nursing home residents. Did he think fourteen and fifteen-year-olds could be comfortable enough in this environment? What would they need to know about writing poetry first? What would they need to know about working with older people, often people who were in pain or uncomfortable? Would the residents feel invaded? He responded with considerable enthusiasm in a note, "Your project sounds wonderful. Could you phone me?"

I had no experience myself with nursing homes and little experience with asking people to write poetry, especially people other than students. I had asked Koch in my letter if he would come to our school, about one hundred miles east of New York City, and do a workshop with my students that would help them prepare for this venture. He thought we could talk about that after he returned from a few months' trip abroad, but in the meantime, he suggested that I investigate possible locations for our work.

Finding a Place

My idea was that we would visit nursing homes once a week for a period of six to eight weeks and that my students would be paired up one-on-one with

an elder person. I had twenty-four students in class, and they were all
willing, if somewhat apprehensive, so I had to find a situation that would
accommodate all of them.

I visited the local senior citizens center, but that did not seem to be the
right place, as the population was transient, and there is a difference
between coming to a place for social activities and a meal for a few hours
each day and actually being a full-time resident of a nursing home. While I
had certainly hoped to be involved in just one place, the closest adult rest
home did not have a large enough population of residents who, the director
felt, would be able to sustain the kind of thought and attention this work
would require. He thought he could suggest about twelve people who
would be interested in participating.

I then asked the director of social activities at a nursing home in a nearby
village if he could come up with another twelve residents whom we could
work with there. He could come close, he thought. No one had attempted
anything of this nature, though, he cautioned. Students sometimes came in
around the holidays to visit, or sing with the group, or bring refreshments,
but no one had come for a sustained time and with a particular purpose,
with some intellectual work in mind.

He had one gentleman in particular, a stroke victim, who had been "very
sharp, involved in intellectual pursuits, an editor at a prestigious national
magazine." The man was depressed and bitter about what had happened to
him, and no one had been able to get him to participate in any of the events
or activities. He described the man as "reclusive" and hoped maybe a young
person could "bring him out" a little.

Between the two places we generated a list of twenty-four residents to
match with my twenty-four ninth graders. Koch had described in *I Never
Told Anybody* some of the health problems that needed to be considered
when asking elderly people to think about and write poetry. He said,
"Some had recent memory loss, were forgetful, tended to ramble a little
when they spoke. Everyone was ill, some people sometimes in pain.
Depression was frequent. A few were blind, and some had serious
problems in hearing" (5). I asked each of the directors to give me some
personality traits and other information that might be useful in matching
my students with the nursing home residents. My notes scribbled on that
list have many associations for me now, but at the time, I had not yet met
any of the residents. Next to their names I wrote comments such as, "Alert;
feisty." "Bright, soft-spoken, difficult articulation due to Parkinson's."
"Character, strong-willed, not inhibited." "Alert, but tires easily, weak due

to coronary condition." "Speech erratic and confusing due to series of small strokes, but very alert mentally."

I wondered if we would be able to do this, and armed with my annotated list of names, genders, personality traits, and ages (they ranged from the late eighties to one resident who was a hundred years old), I discussed possibilities with my students. I asked them to think about whether they'd prefer a woman or a man, whether they'd feel comfortable with someone with a physical handicap, whether they wanted someone "easy" or "a little tough," and we then negotiated the tentative matches. I wonder now what the students were thinking and feeling picturing our venture. They had nothing to go on but a name and a few remarks, and they were agreeing to go into a nursing home—where most had never been—make friends with elderly people, and not just talk with them, but also encourage them to write poetry!

Getting Ourselves Ready

Just before we went on our first visit, Koch conducted a two-hour workshop on a Friday afternoon. He stood in front of the students, tall and bushy-haired, taking a "no-nonsense, this is serious business" approach. In short order, he had these ninth graders all writing poetry. They listened to him read it; noticed how he commented on particular lines, images, and rhythms; and listened to how he structured the questions and assignments to encourage "poetry" instead of prose. He also talked with them about what it might mean to be old, to be living in a nursing/adult home, what he had learned from his own work of having them write poetry, what questions had remained for him from his own experiences. One student reflected, "Mr. Koch explained to me that when they stop working they no longer feel that they are accomplishing anything tangible. They often feel useless and that they cannot contribute anything of value." While Koch addressed their concerns and mine as best he could, he told us that we would learn for ourselves what we needed to know by being sensitive and responsive to the needs and abilities of each person whom we worked with. He encouraged me to keep in touch with him by phone; he would continue to be our "consultant."

Were we nervous? Yes. All of us were. The day before we were to visit the nursing home for the first time, I did an exercise with the class that I frequently use at the beginning of the year with incoming freshmen. It's called "Fear in a Hat." I pass out index cards and ask the students to respond to my questions in a few words or phrases and to number their answers on the cards. They do not put their names on these, and I usually ask four to six questions. I collect the cards and shuffle them well, passing them out again randomly, asking students not to comment on the card they receive, even if by chance they get their own or they recognize the handwriting of another. I then read the questions again, and after each one, we go around the room with students reading the response on the card they've been given. Students have no "claim" on what is read, and no one knows whose thoughts are being expressed. In this way, we get a sense of the feelings of the group without anyone having to admit to a particular "fear." What students hear is that we frequently share the same worries as well as anticipations, and then we can talk about these feelings in the group.

In this case I asked: How do you feel about starting this project? What is the thing you are most worried/concerned about? What do you look forward to the most? What questions do you have? What we learned as we embarked on this new undertaking was that, in general, we were nervous. Would the people like us? Would they want to write poetry? Would they feel ill while we were working with them? What if someone wasn't nice? And yet we were excited—anticipating learning a lot about poetry writing, about life in a nursing home, about aging, about our own abilities to "teach," assist, and be encouraging. We would learn, too, about some of our fears about old people, about challenging our own stereotypes and notions. We were as ready as we were ever going to be, we guessed.

And so we climbed in our yellow school bus the next day and went to the nursing homes. It was new territory for all of us, and I shared my own anxiety, nervousness, and excitement with my students. We were all learning together, and we processed the experience each week on the bus rides home and in class the next day. As the weeks passed, our passion for our project and our confidence in our abilities grew.

Partners Working Together

From the beginning, these ninth graders were compassionate, friendly, and fun. They quickly adapted to the smells and sounds of the nursing homes and were warm and gracious with their new acquaintances. I think now that they were brave to embark on such uncharted territory, but know that each of them embraced this as an opportunity to both learn from and give to others. There is no doubt that some of the matches were more difficult than others.

We established a routine, based on Koch's suggestions, that helped all of us. It was the same process each week. The students collected their partners from their rooms, wheeling them down in their chairs or helping someone with a walker (although many of them who could get themselves there were ready and waiting when we came in). I introduced the theme for the day, read examples, talked about the ideas as I had read and heard Koch model them in *I Never Told Anybody*, as well as in his workshop with us. Sometimes we began with a group "collaborative poem," as Koch had suggested in his book. Each person wrote one line (the residents talked and my students, as Koch and his assistants had, took down what they said), and I would collect these and read them all together as though they were one poem. Then, I would comment on the images, language, rhythm, and sound that I felt worked particularly well. This was an important component of the "teaching" each of us did, and I tried through my comments to the whole group to model for my students ways in which they could encourage the "poet" in their "students." I didn't feel particularly competent to do this well in the beginning, but I felt more comfortable as time went on. As Koch says in *I Never Told Anybody*, "One doesn't have to be an expert in poetry to make such comments, but just to be able to show that one likes something that is funny or beautiful or well said, that makes one remember something or want to laugh or cry" (39). Reading and rereading Koch's descriptions of his work in a nursing home served as my guide throughout our weeks together.

Once our group was warmed up, the ninth graders worked one-on-one for about thirty minutes, generating one or several poems and working on revising as they read the lines back to the poet-resident. At the end of our time, we would always go back to our whole group meeting, where the ninth graders would take turns reading the poetry aloud, and we would listen quietly to the words of memory and feeling that expressed some aspect of the lives the residents had once lived.

Memories

I was always invited to play ball with the bigger
guys in the neighborhood.
I could hold my own with them.
It felt good, because I was the only little guy
    invited to play.
I beamed.

— Tim

The Most Beautiful Thing

The most beautiful thing I ever saw
was my first grandchild.

— Reginald

Music

Music is lovely; it makes me feel young again.
It reminds me of the war; they came home,
        thank God.
I don't want to see any more of them go.

— Eleanor

While we wondered sometimes if reliving some of their memories made them feel sad as they sat in their nursing home chairs so removed from the lives they had once led, we felt that the residents embraced the chance to not only speak of these things but to hear about each other's lives and experiences. Koch says that one of his poets told him that writing poetry made her "feel young again." He comments that "[o]ne thing the poetry gave her, as it gave to all, was a way to talk about life in a way that showed its beauty and its sadness and its humor and, often, because of all that, its value" (50). Sometimes the poems would arise out of prompts I would bring in, such as a vase of red tulips, and we would write about the color, or the flowers, or whatever else the prompt inspired. Poetry gave us all a chance to make sense out of an experience in a new way:

Tulips

My husband had a green thumb and planted
        many flowers.
He planted tulips one year in the garden
so that they bloomed in the form of my name.
My husband and I liked the color red.

— Mary

Blue

Blue is peaceful and pretty
like the sweater that the lady
sitting by the stairs is wearing.
My dress is light blue check.
I had blue eyes and blond hair once.
Of course, now my hair
is white.

— Ellie

We would all applaud when the poems were read, and many of the residents would compliment one another's writing or nod in common remembrance. Listening to the readings at the end gave us a sense of celebration and closure, and I'd again comment on the way a line had been particularly effective or simply repeat phrases that sounded especially good. Then we'd say our goodbyes and board our bus, some of my students laughing together over something that had happened, others sitting quietly gazing out the window, lost in their thoughts.

When our sessions together were over, each student published a booklet of each resident's poems. They experimented with how the lines looked on the page and where the breaks were most effective. They drew titles from the poems themselves. This process also impacted on their own awareness of poetry's force. One student wrote:

> Helping to organize residents' thoughts and phrase responses into clear poems helped my poetry. In the same manner that we encourage detailed responses from our partners, it was necessary to apply [this] to our own poetry. Word choice and organization can have great powers.

Another student commented that she learned to care about what the poem said rather than concentrating too much on the form or the structure. She said, "What I learned from my partner at the nursing home definitely influenced me because the poetry I have written has been centered around the ideas and images."

When the booklets were finished, we went once more for a "poetry party." The students read through the booklets with their partners and picked one poem they wanted to hear in the final read-around. We then heard a reading from each "published" poet, and the booklets were presented to the authors to share with their friends and family. This "Quiet" poem reflects both the power of the poetry and the poignancy of the present life:

Quiet

Quiet is at night right before I go to bed.
Quiet is when I'm mad.
Quiet is just before a storm, the air is heavy,
And you know just when a storm is on its way.
Quiet is here.

Working together with their elderly partners on poems like this prompted reflection in the students. In response to a questionnaire about this project, one student commented:

> This work changed my awareness of age and experience. The old in America are forgotten or—worse—patronized like children—when they are the keepers of a great and wondrous past. The knowledge they have acquired—and wisdom as well—will disappear if it isn't written down—poetry as well as history.

Another student said:

> This poetry writing experience is something I will always remember as a positive experience from high school. My strongest memories were my partner's negative attitude at the start of the project and his change to enthusiasm as he realized he could write poetry.

Although it was not my main intent to teach students about life in a nursing home, being there nonetheless had a powerful and lasting effect on them. In a *Newsday* column entitled "Gray Matters," Saul Friedman quotes from the letter of a friend of a resident in a nursing home in Long Island. The writer, Bill, says:

> I hope you can get people to help these people. It's a bad way to live. It STINKS. After all the years they worked to end up like this. Better in the grave, that's what my friend says. You have to be here to see what's going on" (B9).

Being there let my young students and me understand in a way not otherwise possible the bleakness of institutional living, "when gray days and cold nights seem endless and without form" (B9). What our experience might mean in students' futures when they may have to make decisions about their own elder loved ones, I do not know. I do know they grew in awareness. As one said, "At 14, I rarely had thought about what happens to the elderly when they can no longer take care of themselves." But at least, as many of them reflected in written responses to their work, they were doing something that had positive outcomes for both parties. As Alison wrote, "It made me feel good about myself when the residents looked forward to seeing us every week. It wasn't always about poetry, but communication between two people where we both learned from each other. It was a great experience!" And as Koch told us when he came to our school, "Your writing poetry with them is not to help them to adjust. You're actually changing the situation." Koch told us that we'd be giving the elderly a chance to "make sense out of experience in a new way" and that poetry was "a serious thing for them to work at." My students came to understand, I think, that the work they did was acknowledging the residents intellectual and emotional lives and helping them to utilize these most human capacities by putting those thoughts and feelings into poetry.

Negotiating Logistics

When I tell other teachers about doing this project, as well as two subsequent ones I did later with a day care center and a nursery school, the teachers often say, "This sounds like a planning and scheduling nightmare!" I'm tempted to answer, "It was," but that would not really be true. Moving beyond the walls, working in nontraditional ways, does involve much planning, including numerous phone calls, many checklists, and usually the cooperation of other staff. It also requires a willingness on the part of students to go beyond the normal requirements of class, to make sacrifices, and to take some risks. One must believe that all of this effort will be worth it. These many years later I see the faces of the residents as they heard their words read aloud by the ninth graders at the end of each session, and we all often sat quietly for a moment letting those words and images linger in the air. I hear my students laughing happily as they shared stories on our bus rides home, their fondness for their partners obviously growing with each visit.

Although there were certainly constant changes and rearrangements to be worked out, and these will vary with each school and nursing home setting, I know that this experience affected my teaching profoundly. I realize how capable young people are of crossing boundaries that we, as adults, are often too timid to transgress. And for the residents, what did it mean to finally be able to say out loud, and in poetry, too:

Quiet

Quiet is when I come down stairs and no one says
   hello to me.
Quiet was when two of my children died and
   nobody knew why.
Quiet is when nobody acknowledges my presence
   or knows I'm there.

In titling her book of poetry, *Nobody Knows I'm There* . . . both Lucille, who wrote this poem, and my student Caitlin addressed the isolation many experience in a nursing home. Caitlin wrote in her reflection after doing this project:

> The lady I worked with left a lasting impression on me. She was sweet, kind and very, very lonely. I believe that she had outlived the rest of her family and rarely had interaction with anyone who cared about her while she was in the nursing home. She left me with a

rather bleak outlook on nursing homes, of these places where people waited to die and in the process, acted as if they were already
dead. She was not like that though. She had so much she wanted to
say about the life she had led. Other than me, I do not think she had
anyone to talk to.

Writing Our Own Poems

Caitlin had recorded this "Quiet" poem in a notebook, a black and white
bound volume in which students recorded the poetry the residents wrote.
Each week in the writing center, a room equipped with thirty computers, my
students updated the file of poetry that they were keeping for each resident.
They were also involved during this time writing their own poetry. When
Koch came to visit our class, he had the students writing poems as part of
that workshop. They generated several beginnings that day, which they
wanted to continue working on. Another source for their poetry came from
class each week when we would try out the lesson that we would be
working on with the older people, usually an idea from *I Never Told
Anybody*. This gave the students the chance to experiment with writing the
poems themselves, a practice that gave them more confidence in their own
teaching. For example, before we worked on the "Quiet" theme with the
residents, the students wrote their own "Quiet" poems. Reading these
showed me the great power that working in themes can have. Some of their
"quiet" lines included the following:

> "Quiet is talking to my grandfather in my bed, hoping that he can hear
> me in that way-off place somewhere."
>
> "Quiet was when I found out that my sister had to have an operation."
>
> "It was quiet when my Mom cried, but even quieter when my Dad did."
>
> "It was very quiet when Dad closed our front door for the last time."
>
> "Quiet is when I don't think I've done anything with my life."

I remember that these "quiet" poems in particular generated powerful
images and feelings. These ninth graders experimented with many of the
themes included in *I Never Told Anybody*: colors, memories, favorite things,
music. I wrote along with them but found my own poetry stilted and stylized
compared to their honest and open expressions. One student, who was also
struggling with being more natural, wrote of what she learned from working
with her elder partner, "I was trying too hard to be 'poetic' rather than just

letting things come to mind and writing them down. It made me appreciate my partner's poetry, because it came from his heart." All of us learned from Koch's caution to "Watch out for the words that say, 'Kiss me, I'm poetic.'"

As another way to get them writing their own poetry, I had obtained a class set of Koch's *Sleeping on the Wing*, an anthology of poetry followed by exercises that related to each group of poems. I gave them weekly assignments in this text, so they were writing and typing up poetry from these exercises, too. This system worked very well. One day they would be visiting the nursing homes, and the other they would be in the writing center adding to the files of the person they were matched with as well as refining and adding to their own poetry collections.

Reflections

Looking back on this experience brings the residents' faces and the faces of my students into focus. I see Malcolm holding the hand of the blind gentleman he worked with, both of them smiling while they talk of some memory. I see Jane working so hard to get Liz out of her querulous mood and talk instead about "the most beautiful thing she ever saw." I see Mae so close to Ellie they are almost touching as she strains to hear her and not say "What?" too many times. In the middle of it all, I hear Mabel, with my bright-eyed and laughing Jennie next to her, suddenly yell out, "What is it?! Where am I?" her intense blue eyes shining from where she sits in her wheelchair. I see these young men and women moving easily to the residents' rooms, chatting with them about the past week, and then wheeling or walking them down to our meeting place, the large room where I would begin with a group lesson and then students would take over and begin to work one-on-one to reiterate what the theme or idea was for that day. One young woman wrote to me, five years after the experience, "I had a hard time with my resident. How can I ever forget how miserable she seemed to be there?" Yet she commented also, "Seeing the conditions in which these people lived reminded me of how important it is not to take life for granted. I hope I never end up in a nursing home." Another student commented:

> I can remember the feeling of apprehension. I hadn't had much con-tact with older people because only one grandparent is living. But, after the first few successful poetry sessions, the feeling faded into excitement. I can remember Mary smiling as I came in. That smile would calm my nerves and the 'nursing home' smell became not so strong.

One young man reflected:

> It is a sad and unfortunate aspect of our society that the elderly can
> hold no place in life. When we began working with our partners at
> the home I made many realizations, like that there is a real person
> beneath the wrinkles and age, one very much like myself.

Koch's work assured him that expressing these feelings in poetry did not
make old people feel worse. He speaks of the general belief that the elderly
want quiet and peace and that "these subjects, all having to do with power,
energy and passion, will cause them pain and make them feel empty,
because they will feel unconnected to them . . ." (30). But Koch believes that
both ideas are wrong and that "One's feelings, which are such strong things,
can, even when they are unhappy feelings, go into making something
beautiful" (45). It is not a bad thing to feel strongly, especially when that
feeling can be channeled into art. "Passion and energy is what life is all
about," says Koch, and I wonder if bringing them out in a nursing home can
be about letting life back in.

Our weekly visits were both exhausting and exhilarating. Again and again
I was moved by the patience, care, and seriousness with which each of my
students approached this work. The joy came from the relationships we
formed and, finally, the magic of the poetry. The music it created for our ears
each week! The opportunity it gave all of us to see familiar things anew and
to hear combinations of words we hadn't thought of. As Koch says, it's not
only the poet who is made richer through the writing, but the reader and
listener, too. When I think about the impulse that led me to engage my
students and myself in this work, I go back to Koch's words that inspired me:

> Still, it is such a pleasure to say things, and such a special kind of
> pleasure to say them as poetry. I didn't, when I began, think much
> about the problems. I started, instead, with my feeling for the plea-
> sure people could find in writing poetry, and assumed I could deal
> with any problems as they came up. (*I Never Told Anybody* 6)

That we as students and teachers were able to help people engage in the
pleasure of "saying things" was a powerful and affecting experience for all of
us. We did not focus on the "Why not?" but instead on the "What if?" And
we were doubly enriched, for there is great pleasure in doing something
good, and the poetry the students and their partners created gave us all
moments of beauty and delight and laughter and pause. They were bright
spots in our days.

Works Cited

Friedman, Saul. "Gray Matters." *Newsday* 28 Dec. 1996: B9.
Koch, Kenneth. *I Never Told Anybody*. New York: Random House, 1977.

14 Assessing the Teaching and Learning of Poetry

Albert B. Somers

"Pass/Fail" is a poem by Linda Pastan about the dream that often disturbs the sleep of former college students (I've had it many times). In the dream as well as the poem, the student is scheduled for a test in a course he has never taken. The test looms ahead just out of reach, imposing and inescapable, "waiting to be failed." It is the classic Catch-22, and the only way out is waking up.

"Pass/Fail" is one of the few poems written about tests and examinations. *The Columbia Granger's Index to Poetry* doesn't even assign the subject a heading. Is assessment, one wonders, unworthy of consideration by poets? Are future poets permanently traumatized in school by true-false items and essay questions? Are poetry and testing mutually exclusive realms?

Whatever the concerns, poetry *is* an element of the English language arts curriculum, and is, as such, like spelling, reading for inference, and vocabulary, subject to assessment. At least, it is subject to be considered for assessment.

Some would say our work with poetry should not be evaluated at all. In her article, "Poets on Teaching Poetry," Diane Lockward quotes Lois Harrod on the subject: "the worst thing a teacher could do with one of [my] poems would be to put it on a multiple choice test." Of a similar misgiving by another poet, Marie Howe, Lockward says, "When I reminded [Howe] that English teachers have to produce grades, she suggested that we ask students to bring in poems they like and write about one of them. This could be a poem already discussed in class, a different one by a poet whose other

Reprinted from *Teaching Poetry in High School* by Albert B. Somers.

works have been studied, or one by a poet not covered in class" (1994, 65–66).

So, we entertain another question: How much about the teaching and learning of poetry should we try to evaluate and what forms should such evaluation take?

Traditional Assessment

Just for fun, read the following poem "The Whipping" by Robert Hayden. Read it two or three times. Then complete the following test.

The Whipping

The old woman across the way
    is whipping the boy again
and shouting to the neighborhood
    her goodness and his wrongs.

Wildly he crashes through elephant ears,
    pleads in dusty zinnias,
while she in spite of crippling fat
    pursues and corners him.

She strikes and strikes the shrilly circling
    boy till the stick breaks
in her hand. His tears are rainy weather
    to woundlike memories:

My head gripped in bony vise
    of knees, the writhing struggle
to wrench free, the blows, the fear
    worse than blows that hateful

Words could bring, the face that I
    no longer knew or loved. . . .
Well, it is over now, it is over,
    and the boy sobs in his room,

And the woman leans muttering against
    a tree, exhausted, purged —
avenged in part for lifelong hidings
    she has had to bear.

Example Test 1

1. "The Whipping" was written by _____.
2. True or False: "The Whipping" is about a boy who shoplifts.
3. The speaker in the poem is
   a. the old woman
   b. the boy who was whipped
   c. an observer of the whipping
   d. the principal of the boy's school
4. True or False: The speaker in the poem was himself once whipped.
5. True or False: The old woman in the poem has herself been a victim.

If necessary, go back and check your answers against the poem. You probably did pretty well. On the other hand, what does a score of, say, 80 percent on a test like this prove? Is this what we want our students to be able to demonstrate at the end of a poetry unit? I would hope not—for at least three reasons: (1) the test assesses facts alone; (2) in its focus on facts, it depends on recall of literal information; and (3) it requires no thoughtful development of an extended response.

As an alternative, consider another test. A teacher spends three weeks on poetry, follows all the guidelines and suggestions offered in earlier chapters of this book (she is indeed exemplary), and presents the following written assessment on day 15:

Example Test 2

Directions: We have spent the last three weeks reading and discussing and studying numerous poems, many of your own selection. We have talked at length about some of the ideas that poets write about and some of the techniques that they use. On this test, choose *one* of the following three new poems *[they would be attached]* and complete *each* of the following exercises:

1. Write five questions that would encourage you to think about one of the poem's themes, to consider the meaning, the "point."
2. Explain how the poet has used one of the concepts we have studied. Explain in particular how the concept is used to reinforce the poem's meaning.

By almost any measure, this is better than *Example Test 1*. For one thing, it offers students choices—not only one of the three poems, but their choice of questions to formulate and a concept in the poem to write about. Also, this test operates on a higher level than the first: it asks students to apply what they have learned to a poem they have not discussed in class.

In my view, this second test is a justifiable kind of assessment of the knowledge students learn about poetry—*as long as a few critical requirements are met*:

1. The students have been thoroughly prepared to take the test. In this case, it would mean a good deal of previous class discussion of several poems in which idea and theme are revealed and much attention given to selected poetic concepts. Moreover, students would have had previous opportunities to develop sets of questions around a variety of poems, perhaps in small groups for the members of others groups or the entire class to respond to.

2. The "materials" the students are to work with—the three new poems—are selected with utmost care, particularly in terms of accessibility and relevance.

3. The students are intellectually prepared for the kinds of mental operations required by the test, in this case for the most part, application.

Several efforts have been made by psychologists over the years to describe the various levels of learning or intellectual functioning, perhaps none more widely known and used than Bloom's taxonomy. As most teachers know, the levels or stages of Bloom's hierarchy in order of complexity are *knowledge (recall), comprehension, application, analysis, synthesis,* and *evaluation.* Applied to "The Whipping," a teacher's use of the taxonomy to generate test items might yield the following questions (which are similar to those presented on the same poem in Chapter 6):

> Knowledge: Where does the poem take place? Is the old woman angry? *(The student recalls the answers from the text of the poem.)*
>
> Comprehension: Explain who you think the speaker is. *(The student expresses an inferred answer in her own words.)*
>
> Application: Do you think the situation would have been different if the old woman had been well educated (assuming for a moment that she wasn't)? *(In responding, the student applies what he knows to a new situation.)*

Analysis: Explain the varied use of punctuation marks by the poet. *(The student responds after examining how commas, a colon, an ellipsis, and dash function in the poem.)*

Synthesis: If you had to predict, what kind of parent do you think "the boy" will become, especially considering line 19? *(The student projects—in effect, creates—a hypothetical outcome.)*

Evaluation: Do you think the shift in point of view in lines 13–18 is clear—or confusing? Is this a good poem? *(The student makes judgements based on established criteria.)*

It could be argued, of course, that the latter questions in the set are more demanding and thus more worthy of placing on a test, but this determination would depend on the teacher's response to the first and third conditions. Even when we acknowledge the superiority of *Example Test 2,* any teacher knows that a major problem remains: the test will take a lot of time to grade. The only way to address the challenge of testing on higher levels of thought while cutting down on grading time is to include on any test, along with an essay question or two, a section of objective questions that demand more than recall.

Imagine, for example, a teacher who has just taught a three-week unit in which she placed a good deal of emphasis on the concepts of speaker, figurative language, sound, and theme. She wants in some way to evaluate the extent to which the students have a grasp on those concepts. To do this, the teacher could include a poem the students haven't read (like the following, which *we* first saw in Chapter 4) along with the accompanying questions:

Example Test 3

Flying at Night

Above us, stars. Beneath us, constellations
Five billion miles away, a galaxy dies
like a snowflake falling on water. Below us,
some farmer, feeling the chill of that distant death,
snaps on his yard light, drawing his sheds and barn
back into the little system of his care.
All night, the cities, like shimmering novas,
tug with bright streets at lonely lights like his.

— Ted Kooser

Directions: Complete the following five questions in response to the above poem:

1. The speaker in this poem is most likely (a) a farmer; (b) a pilot; (3) an alien; or (4) an astronomer.

2. The phrase "like a snowflake" is a (1) metaphor; (2) paradox; (3) simile; or (4) symbol.

3. Of the following lines, which one has an example of alliteration? (1) line 2; (2) line 3; (3) line 5; or (4) line 8.

4. Of the following, which one is the best reason for placing the alliteration in that line?

   a. to make the line sound lighter

   b. to make the line sound heavier

   c. to emphasize the line

5. Of the following, which one do you think best expresses the theme of the poem?

   a. Even though we may seem alone, we are drawn together by mutual caring.

   b. Rural life is better than city life.

   c. The sky at night is beautiful, but it reminds us of how insignificant we are.

By having students apply their knowledge to this new poem, the teacher has tested well above the level of recall. Yet this part of the test would take, for each student, no more than fifteen seconds to grade. I would complete the test by adding an essay question like this:

> From your folder of poems that you like, choose one to illustrate your response to *one* of the following statements:
>
> (1) Imagery in a poem helps the reader vividly see, hear, and feel the speaker's experience.
>
> (2) The speaker in a poem is not necessarily the poet.
>
> (3) Metaphor in a poem often helps us to understand the poet's intended point or meaning.

With traditional testing, then, my approach would be to design a test that counts between 15 and 25 percent of the unit grade. On the test, I would develop several higher-level questions around a new poem and at least one essay question. Such a test achieves several ends: (1) in part, it tests above the knowledge level; (2) it requires the writing of one essay response; and (3) it reduces to some degree the time required for grading.

Even with an assessment like *Example Test 3*, the teaching of poetry will often call for other kinds of evaluation besides tests to account for the unit's additional 75–85 percent. At times, rating scales, checklists, and other devices can be created and used. Here are two examples:

Rating Scale for Original Poems

Originality

|_____/_____/_____/_____/_____/_____/
    poor   fair   good   excellent

Clarity

|_____/_____/_____/_____/_____/_____/

Use of imagery

|_____/_____/_____/_____/_____/_____/

Use of figurative language

|_____/_____/_____/_____/_____/_____/

Compression of expression

|_____/_____/_____/_____/_____/_____/

Mechanics

|_____/_____/_____/_____/_____/_____/

The teacher would present the scale well in advance of the writing of poems and make certain that students understood the six criteria. If she wished (I wouldn't), she could assign numbers across the scale (1 to 6) and thus achieve a numerical rating, perhaps with ranges of resulting grades (e.g., 34–36 = A, 31–33 = B, etc.). She could even double the numbers for criteria she wanted to weigh more heavily, e.g., assigning Originality a range of 2 through 12 instead of 1 through 6.

Checklist for Small Group Multimedia Presentation of a Poem

( ) 1. At least three pieces of equipment were used in the presentation.

( ) 2. Each piece of equipment was used effectively.

( ) 3. The poem was presented both aurally and visually.

( ) 4. Each member of the group was involved in the presentation.

( ) 5. Other relevant points.

Here the teacher simply indicates with a check (✓) whether or not each criterion is met.

Authentic Assessment

Even acknowledging the effectiveness of *Example Test 3*, there remain many poets and teachers among us who would prefer that assessment of the teaching and learning of poetry include no tests at all. Instead, if there must be evaluation, they would argue for some version that falls under the umbrella of *authentic assessment.*

Authentic assessment, of course, represents an effort to evaluate students' ability to *use* knowledge or skills in real or simulated settings that more closely mirror the demands of "real life" (hence the word *authentic*).[1] As such, the approach is ongoing and individualized. It informs students at the outset of the standards and of how their performance will be judged. Thus, it involves students in the evaluation process. Authentic assessment often makes use of products, projects, or performances. For any given student, the organizational system is often a *portfolio*, a collection of work developed and maintained by the student and presented for consideration at various stages during a unit or some other period of time. When the student and his teacher decide that the portfolio is ready for assessment, the process often involves several people, certainly the two of them, but possibly other teachers, an administrator, even a parent or a person from the community (maybe a poet!).

In a poetry unit, a portfolio of work might include some of the following items (each followed here with examples of criteria to be used):

> (1) *a folder of poems the student likes, some with written reasons for her preferences*
>
> Criteria: total number of poems, evidence of breadth of search, evidence of maturity in appreciation (e.g., poems that do not rhyme in addition to some that do), evidence of enthusiasm for particular favorites
>
> Criteria for written explanations: clarity, detail, conciseness, absence of errors

(2) *a collection of original poems as well as the draft versions of those poems; the student might select two or three for final evaluation*

Criteria: originality, clarity, compression of thought, vividness of language, use of selected forms and techniques, absence of errors in mechanics

(3) *a set of critiques of selected poems, with one or two highlighted*

Criteria: quality of thought, reference to (use of) concepts studied, variety of poems critiqued, quality of writing

(4) *an annotated collection of Internet sites on poetry that the student has found interesting or useful either to himself or to a given audience (e.g., a poetry teacher)*

Criteria: variety of sites, quality of sites, evidence of effort, accuracy of URLs (Web site addresses), quality of writing in the annotations

(5) *drawings or paintings to accompany one or more favorite poems accompanied by explanations of choices and purposes*

Criteria: quality of the art work (to be judged by an art teacher), quality of writing in the explanations

(6) *the oral reading of a number of selected poems*

Criteria: quality of performance in terms of appropriateness of intonation, volume,pronunciation, and pace; number and variety of poems selected

(7) *the performance of a poem (perhaps involving other students): choral reading, mime, dance, reader's theater, etc.*

Criteria: originality of performance, quality of performance, depth of interpretation

(8) *a multimedia presentation of a selected poem*

Criteria: variety of media used, quality of presentation (continuity, clarity, etc.)

(9) *a bibliography of works on a selected favorite poet*

Criteria: length of bibliography, variety of sources consulted, accuracy of citations

(10) *a research study of a selected poet or poem*

Criteria: number and quality of sources consulted, effectiveness in use of resources(integration of more than one into a single paragraph, etc.), quality of writing, accuracy of citations

The student would work with his teacher in advance to select those projects he prefers as well as a schedule of stages and deadlines. The two would work together, meeting at regular intervals so the student could receive adequate ongoing feedback. Ideally, authentic assessment promotes not only ongoing assessment, but also the development of the student's ability to evaluate his or her own performance. The use of grades is discouraged, although they can be accommodated.

As a poetry teacher, I would use authentic assessment. I like its emphasis on gradual improvement, on the student having a voice, on the development of a close working relationship between teacher and student, and on the student's growth in evaluating his or her own work. It all makes a lot of sense. Still, I'm not sure I'm ready to assign traditional testing to the ashheap. There would be times, I think, when I'd like to see what my students could do with poetry on a pencil-and-paper test.

So I would use both approaches. Just as I would choose both Orchestrator and Facilitator as classroom personas (Chapter 5), here with assessment I would be both innovative and conventional. I'd be "authentic," but occasionally, I think, I'd toss in a test, one that was fair and reliable, that encouraged my students to think, that required them to defend their ideas and opinions in writing—and that led to the demise of the intimidating "Pass/Fail" dream in Linda Pastan's poem.

Note

1. Synonymous terms include *performance-based assessment*, *alternative assessment*, and *portfolio assessment*.

15 At Home with Poetry: Constructing Poetry Anthologies in the High School Classroom

Anthony J. Scimone

Nothing about the teaching of English requires restraint as much as the teaching of poetry. Most teachers will readily grant that students can independently read short and long fiction, drama, and contemporary nonfiction, but when it comes to verse, we are reluctant to allow our students to experience it on their own terms, unmediated by the teacher's word. In my own practice, the reason for this was quite simple. My students' general lack of familiarity with poetry formed a vacuum that I was sorely tempted to fill. And yet, if I believed that literary discovery rather than literary information was at the center of imaginative learning, I would have to allow even unsophisticated readers to make some of their own choices.

Inventing a Structure

My first challenge in putting theory into practice was to define an assignment that allowed students to make these choices. Much of what I wanted them to do was traditional—for example, explaining how figurative language works—but I also wanted them to make their own selections, to talk about what they thought separated a good poem from a bad one, to make connections beyond the text, and to envision a meaningful thematic overview that would provide a context for all of their work. I wanted too much, certainly too much for my usual class discussion approach. Besides,

Reprinted from *English Journal*, November 1999.

the problem wasn't only their lack of sophistication as readers; these were passive students. Ultimately, it was this passivity that got to me.

If I wanted them to budge even a little, I would have to begin by asking them to construct their own learning. An essay or poster or group presentation wouldn't accommodate all of my objectives, but a book would. Asking tenth grade students to create a book about something as foreign to them as poetry seemed like a dubious request. I would have to give considerable thought to the criteria for success if this venture were to have value.

I began with what was easiest. The end product ought to be attractive and appealing, but not childish. I collected a few anthologies and pricey textbooks. Typically, they featured recognizable works of art, some of which were familiar to my students. Monet, Degas, and other Impressionists seemed to be favored. I secretly hoped that some students would attempt their own illustrations and visual interpretations of poetry, but those who had little artistic ability were encouraged to use photographs or magazine pictures. The visual effect of this book could also be enhanced by including a variety of materials: sheet music, computer-generated graphics, photographs, and abstract design.

I generally regarded this "artistic" aspect of a project as too soft, too superficial for capable students who needed more, not less, academic rigor in high school. But what emerged surprised me. Gradually, they became aware that they were investing time and effort in the creation of something that reflected them, and their concern extended beyond appearance. The final products gave evidence of greater care with mechanics, multiple revisions, text that was attractively typed with few typographical errors, and language that was more precise and more sophisticated than anything my students had previously written. I came to realize that this aspect of the project, which I had regarded as least important, instilled a pride of authorship.

Content and Criteria

Initially, my assignment to create a poetry book was met with considerable skepticism and a great many questions about what should be included. Suggesting viable options and insisting on certain common elements was a critical step. All books would have to contain a preface that defined the focus of what was to follow. The poems, preferably between five and ten, would be the core of the book. Some discussion of at least three of the poems was also required. These responses were kept simple. Each contained an interpretation; examples of figurative language, tone, and diction that the students thought were especially effective; and a personal reaction to the poem. This last part often caused students to relax the formality of analytic writing. For example, writing about Marge Piercy's "Barbie Doll," Jackie says the poem "is a rebuttal to men who expect many of the things mentioned in the poem," and that although "a woman can be anything she wants such as a doctor, lawyer or teacher, she is still expected to have cookies waiting for her children when they come home from school." These commentaries could be kept together and presented after the poem, or they might be structured in whatever way the student thought would work best: personal response, poem, interpretation, or discussion of poetic technique.

I also gave my students plenty of other suggestions intended to open up their thinking about particular themes as well as the overall effect of the book. They were encouraged to include song lyrics that reflected parallel ideas, background information on a particular poet or historical incident, plenty of visuals to entice readers, and news articles or stories that further informed their purpose. In a few books, even original poetry appeared.

The criteria by which all of this work could be evaluated was based on the same design I had used for term papers. The familiar categories of meaning, development, organization, and technical control would appear, but with added language to help define my expectations. The rubric, which we spent almost an entire period discussing, was not intended to be a scoring form for the teacher, but a student-friendly document that invited questions. We returned to it continuously during the process (I recommend having many copies on hand), and it became my comment sheet at the end of the project. (See Figure 1 on p. 186.)

As one might imagine, the students had many questions about what I meant by "effectively," "professionally," and "inventive." I reminded them that this was not an assignment, but an original book worthy of publication, and each day I would horrify them with "a great idea" for going public. I would display their books in the writing center, use them as models in future years, show them to other teachers at a regional convention, perhaps even write an article about them! They groaned outwardly, but with each passing day, they also showed greater care for their own work and more interest in selecting and reading poetry. I knew almost immediately that helping them to understand and meet the criteria would be more valuable (and for me more enjoyable) than the more static writing process I had used in the past. And throughout the three to four weeks it took to research, draft, revise, and publish, I still had many opportunities to present my own favorite poems and "model" what I wanted them to do.

By far, however, the most important and successful element of the project was the preface. Asked to write an opening statement that explained not only the theme but the reasons for making particular choices, students often adopted a tone that was reflective about the larger issues being addressed, as well as the nature of poetry itself. While much of the commentary was unsophisticated, many students arrived at an apprehension of poetry as the best way to express certain kinds of human experience. In her book on the poetry of animals, Beth wonders whether our recurring interest in using animals as metaphors is because they remind us of ourselves and we want to know more about who we are. She becomes even more philosophical and complex as she ponders how poets use animals in comparisons that help explore the human experience.

Student Selections and Response

I was surprised by the poetic content of these student-created books, as well as the commentary that accompanied the choices. Above all, what distinguished these "books" from the flat, pro forma poetry papers I had assigned in previous years was a student voice that was richer, more genuine, and more engaging. In the preface to his book, *Poetry of the Civil War*, Kevin writes:

> War is one of the most horrid examples of human greed and folly. Fathers and brothers are taken away, their lives randomly selected for the sacrifice. The carnage is too much for anyone to comprehend; yet mankind still tries to characterize it, explain it and describe the toll it takes upon people. The poems in this selection are all based upon the Civil War, doubtless, the United States' most devastating and tedious conflict. These poems reflect the ideas of poets who were affected by the great magnitude and emotional impact of the war.

Kevin's book included Whitman's "Ashes of Soldiers" and "Ode to the Confederate Dead" by Allen Tate, works that I probably would have considered too challenging for a class reading.

As I reread this, I can't help but remember that Kevin was the same boy who needed an inordinate amount of hand-holding throughout the year, only to produce unimaginative, formulaic introductions. Convincing tenth grade students that writing has to be informed by purpose never seems more difficult than when I am asked, "How many sentences do we have to have in a paragraph?" Yet recasting this assignment into a book seems to have broadened imaginative possibilities. When I suggested that the most original books sought to define not just a theme but a special angle, Robert took his idea from Langston Hughes and created a book entitled *Dreams Deferred*. His preface begins with some research on the nature of dreams and ends with the observation that dreams are a way to overcome prejudice and inequality. He also points out that the stories of dreamers might constitute an escape but might also be an expression of pride, achievement, and determination. Robert's search took him beyond the obvious choices, and I thought it quite remarkable that he found "kitchenette building" by Gwendolyn Brooks. Even more remarkable was the direction he chose, since he was famous for his provocative remarks in class about minorities who expected to have everything given to them. Privately, I wondered why the boy who had expressed such reactionary ideas in one forum was suddenly a model of multicultural sensitivity. Was there one Robert who played to the crowd and a different one who set ideas down in the more durable format of a book that might reflect on its creator?

Teacher Reflection

I think my instincts in designing a lesson are often right, but it would be disingenuous to suggest that I anticipated as much from this assignment as I got. I was genuinely surprised by the work my students produced, and I think they were surprised that poetry was accessible to them. I have a better sense now of which aspects of these poetry books were best; most important of all, I have models to help me introduce the assignment in the future. I also have ideas about what to add. For one thing, the absence of an oral component is conspicuous; the display of the student books could have been an opportunity for sharing ideas and practicing interpretive reading.

There is also something in this process that I can't quite trace; something in the student responses suggests a stepping back from reading and writing as just a classroom task. There is a level of engagement that lends larger vision and engenders a willingness to make meaning rather than find answers.

Ironically, I have created assignments that are somewhat similar, but less successful, with my Advanced Placement seniors. Drama portfolios and collections of writings in response to several short works of fiction have not had the same unity or cohesion as the tenth grade poetry books. Too often, I see individual analyses that are superb, but there's a failure to conceive of the collection as a whole. These portfolios are not enlivened by the same creative purpose and regrettably remain simply good examples of academic writing. No doubt, adjusting my pedagogical approach by putting greater emphasis on reflection and synthesis will go a long way toward solving this problem. But there is also something special about the experience of reading poetry.

On the one hand, poetic language and syntax create enormous obstacles for some students, but unlike longer genres, poems can be glanced at, set aside, reread, and examined alongside other poems. Students can literally arrange these short texts on a table in front of them, relying more on a nimble eye than on memory. A sense of comparison and connection emerges more easily. A reader would require a considerable breadth of knowledge and literary experience to examine five works of fiction for their similarities. Not so with poetry, where even a tenth grade student can derive enough confidence and enough comfort to want to read on. Michael, in *Aim High*, his book on the poetry of running, seemed to get this idea. In his response to "Strategy for a Marathon" by Marnie Mueller he says this:

> The tone of this is one of optimism. It's the positive outlook, the confidence that keeps the runner going past the halfway mark and right to home. Home to a runner is the finish line. The place we call home is where we have a sense of warmth, pride, and above all accomplishment. It's what keeps runners running and students studying.

The books I asked my students to construct served as a means to order and enhance their thinking, but the greatest benefit may have been a construction of themselves as readers at home with poetry.

	highly proficient	proficient	satisfactory	needs work
MEANING: Interpretations are clearly expressed and persuasively defended; your individual analyses must demonstrate a consistent reading and must be relevant to the book's theme.				
DEVELOPMENT: Examples from the texts are selected and cited carefully; figurative language, tone, and diction are discussed in terms of the overall interpretation; personal reactions are included for each poem.				
ORGANIZATION: Individual commentaries are organized with a clear beginning, middle, and end; ideas progress logically and in a manner that is easy to follow; the sections of your book are arranged effectively.				
TECHNICAL CONTROL & APPEARANCE: Since this book is intended for public display, hold yourself to a zero tolerance policy on errors; edit your own work and enlist others to help proofread your draft for errors in wording, sentence structure, spelling, punctuation, etc. Your cover and additional materials should reflect you; be inventive, imaginative, and think like the writer of a book, not a student!				

Figure 1. Criteria for Evaluation.

*This book was set in Optima and Trajan by
City Desktop Productions.
The typeface used on the cover was Trajan.
The book was printed by IPC Communication Services.*